THE EMAIL
lifestyle

RITOBAN CHAKRABARTI

First Edition

ISBN: 1512089273
ISBN-13: 978-1512089271

www.emailinstruments.com

To Mom and Dad

For your immense support - through good times and bad

PART ONE
My Story

INTRODUCTION

I COULD HEAR the waves crashing against the rusty pillars that supported the magnificent structure standing proudly at the edge of the island. Yet another honeymooning couple stared at me blankly while I hammered away at the keys of my laptop.

I had come to this isolated island in the middle of the Indian Ocean to get away from the crowd and to write my first novel. It was a daunting task, which became even more difficult when people stared at the only loner at the resort.

I put on my headphones and turned up the volume. I wanted to drown out the judgement and focus on working. It wasn't that difficult and within minutes I had another paragraph typed out. The corner of my eye couldn't help but notice that couple staring way too blankly. I had to ask.

"First time in Maldives?"

Silence.

A lot of newlyweds head off to Maldives for their honeymoon and the island resort where I was staying came highly recommended on TripAdvisor. It's a global honeymooning destination and I couldn't expect everyone at that resort to understand English.

The guy smiled and replied back in a broken Spanish accent.

"Yes. What... uh... about you?"

"Same, same. I came here alone to write a book."

"Oh! That's nice!"

Everyone likes creative people. If you do something out of the norm, then people look at you differently. Also if you come to a romantic resort alone.

"Where are you from?" I asked, hoping to strike up a conversation.

I talked to the Portuguese guy for several hours. The wife didn't understand English, so she chose to watch YouTube videos on her iPad. In between stories of Brazil, drinks being exchanged, and a FaceTime call from their kids in Portugal, he asked me a question.

"So what do you do?"

This age-old question got me thinking. Whenever you're at a party or meeting someone new, you inevitably get asked this dreaded question. I almost always would reply back, "I'm an internet marketer".

This would instantly end the conversation because, let's face it, no one likes talking about a profession they don't understand.

But this time was different. Travelling alone is enlightening. Here I was, alone in an amazing resort sipping some Brazilian cocktail, working on my passion project without a care in the world—and it was a Thursday.

I looked out at the dark rippling horizon and couldn't help but feel blessed to be in an industry where big money is made simply by executing your passion projects. Where there are no weekdays or weekends—you work whenever you want to. Where the people you talk to reside in GChat and Skype. Where you can pay off for an exotic island resort vacation simply by typing a few words and hitting the 'Send' button.

I like to call myself an *experimental* internet marketer simply because I like trying out new things. I guess this ideology stemmed from my childhood when I believed the only way to live a good life was to be a jack of all trades and master of none.

PPC, SEO, Web Development, Graphic Design, Programming, Social Media, AdWords, AdSense, Webinars, PPV, CPA. If you can think of an internet marketing activity, I've probably done it. I've been successful with a lot of campaigns and failed with even more. But there's one thing I've learnt.

Nothing beats Email Marketing.

If you have an online business or if your business is online—you need Email Marketing. It has stood the test of time and millions of businesses worldwide leverage its power daily. There's no better way of spreading your message.

If you have an email address, then you're probably subscribed to one if not several email lists. Even if you think you're not subscribed to any list, think about this:

When you signed up with Gmail and got your shiny new email address, then you got subscribed to Google's list. You gave Google permission to send you important announcements and notification emails.

Do you have a Facebook account? What did they ask you when you signed up? Yeah, your email address.

What about Amazon? What about all those dozens, if not hundreds of websites where you entered your email address either to get something for free or to sign up for a service?

You've been exposed to Email Marketing from the first day you had an email address. There's a reason your email address is more valuable to companies than your real name.

An email address is your identity. It's the equivalent of a Social Security number in the online world. It identifies YOU.

And you keep checking your email account on a daily basis. So you've given businesses the privilege of sending you a daily or weekly email.

There's a much bigger reason why your email address is so valuable.

An email address is worth $1 per month to an Email Marketer. This figure varies greatly with the niche and the marketing strategy of the company— but for all us peeps in the Email Marketing world, the safe number is $1 per month.

I've seen some active marketers make as much as $3 per month per subscriber.

So the next time you get someone to give you their email address—know that you're adding $1/ month to your bottom line.

The word 'Email' might mean something different to you. Most people use it to stay in touch with family and friends, for official communications or to check Facebook notifications. But it means something completely different to me.

Owning a list of people who have given you permission to email them is the best asset anyone could have. It's better than property, company stock, cars, gadgets, you name it.

An email list is your identity, a way of communicating your message to people who are genuinely interested in hearing what you have to say. It's a one-to-many interaction that allows you to enrich people's lives both professionally and personally.

I have sold more than $4 million online with a big chunk of that BECAUSE of email marketing, I feel truly grateful and blessed. However, it wasn't always like this.

MY HOME OFFICE

YOU SEE, I'M from India. I've spent my entire life here and intend to spend the rest of it here. India is a colourful and vibrant country where the richest rich and the poorest poor reside, hundreds of languages are spoken, and proponents of every religion practice their beliefs. India is truly a diverse nation with infinite beauty in nature and purity in souls.

But India is also a place where electricity keeps cutting off ever so frequently, where the internet speeds a decade ago were comparable to dial-up connections, and where parents decide their kids' futures.

I got started online on a warm summer day in 2006 with a 0.2 Mbps internet connection, on an old and frustratingly slow Compaq desktop that sat on top of a little desk in my parents' house. I was barely making it through my engineering college—having opted into the computer science stream. I actually thought I would be an expert coder after my engineering degree. Oh, I was so naïve. We were taught old technologies that didn't matter in the modern world. We never even touched HTML.

HTML! It's the basis of every webpage, and no one in my batch had any idea what it meant.

So yes, I was not in an ideal situation. But that's when the magic happens. You put someone with a will to fight in a tight corner and he will show you how to break out of the corner, step out in the real world, and embrace it.

I love creating new things. Ever since I was a child, I had this knack to think out of the box and make something new. Mom told me that when I was in tenth grade, I had created an animation of stick people running away from a bomb that was apparently quite hilarious. I didn't remember ever creating that, but Mom certainly did. When we were given clay dough to make a standard cup in fourth grade, I was the only one experimenting with the cup design. The rest of the class tried mimicing the model cup the teacher had placed in front of us.

So when I came across the beautiful world of web designing, I saw an infinite sea of creativity. I could mix and match a dozen things and create something new out of it.

I spent the most of my first year online creating HTML pages—sometimes on Yahoo Geocities, sometimes on my computer. I learned about a new CMS out there called 'Joomla', which was much more popular at the time than WordPress. It made the entire website creation process too darn easy, with templates and extensions and what not.

But after about a year of experimenting and learning, I realized I should start making money leveraging this creativity. I was sure there were people out there who would pay good money to get their websites created. Bear in mind, I don't belong to a business background. My brother is a doctor, my dad's a doctor, and my mom's a school teacher. All three are highly skilled and reputed in their fields—but still no inclination whatsoever towards business.

I knew I was treading a path that would lead to some family issues but I went with it anyway.

My logic was if I could make money doing what I love doing—that right there is the dream come true.

I found out about freelancing websites. Scriptlance (since acquired by Freelancer) was all the rage back then. Clients would come to Scriptlance, post their requirement, and us freelancers had to place our bid and convince the client to hire us. After a few failed bids, I started observing the kind of messaging other bidders were using and the kind of bids that became the winning bids. I noticed the freelancers with plenty of 5star reviews got hired real quickly.

So I changed my strategy and started bidding real low. I needed to get as many projects (read: reviews) under my belt as possible—even if it meant I had to slave away.

And slave away I did. I still remember I had a project where the client paid me $5 for eight hours of intensive coding work. Eight hours. Five dollars.

But I started getting great reviews because clients loved my work and I started getting plenty of projects. The best thing was I was LEARNING on the job.

I didn't know diddly about many of the projects I undertook. But I was confident I would learn and leverage Google's massive knowledge.

Bear in mind, it took about 10 seconds to load a Google search result way back then with the dead slow internet connection.

But all this working during college alienated me from friends and society. I rarely hung out with friends after college. I skipped several parties because I wanted to work instead. I woke up in the morning, headed over to college, listened to lectures, logged in to the college computer and worked there, came back home and worked till I fell asleep.

Yes, I fell asleep on the desk several times.

I have no regrets. I wouldn't be here if it weren't for that time.

I learnt web designing, graphic designing, programming, web development and a whole lot more that year.

The first floor of my parents' house was my abode and that Compaq computer had paid for itself several times over.

It had been two years now, and I had started making a decent amount of money with freelancing but it wasn't enough. I knew I could use my creativity to make way more.

That was also the time when we had campus placements in college and one of the largest IT companies came recruiting. I cleared all the rounds, but told my interviewer I would only take the job if they placed me on a much higher pay scale than the rest of the batch. They were paying out $300 a month, and I was already making three times that amount.

When they announced the results, they specially mentioned that the HR manager needed to talk to me. So I went and explained him 'the situation'. Little did I know his hands were tied and he wasn't authorized to offer a higher pay package. So I calmly excused myself, rejecting their job offer. I still remember everyone in that room got weirded out by what I was saying—felt good to be different from the crowd.

But now I had more pressure than ever before to make something out of this online business thingy because I had rejected the job offer that most of my colleagues had accepted. I HAD to make this work.

That's when Warrior Forum came into my life, which is the largest internet marketing forum. (Again, it was acquired by Freelancer, but only recently.)

I became a part of several discussions and learnt a lot from other marketers' experiences. I bought plenty of Warrior Special Offers (WSO's) and learned from them.

I decided to quit freelancing completely because of one simple formula that haunted me. The amount of money I made with freelancing ALWAYS would be directly proportional to the number of hours I put in. So if I didn't work for one day, I would make nothing that day.

I wanted automation. I wanted more control over my revenue without the need to slave away.

My strong suit was that I actually went ahead and IMPLEMENTED all the strategies I learned. All of them. One of the courses taught about launching your own product. I realized since I had so much knowledge about Joomla, I should create a product around that.

So I spent the next few weeks building themes and extensions that would make a nice little product. I learnt how to write sales copy, how to list my product on ClickBank, how to get affiliates to promote my product, and a whole lot more.

A lot of this learning was just like cream floating on top of boiled milk. I had absolutely no contacts in the industry and no way to drive affiliate connections. I relied completely on word-of-mouth.

I waited for several days and nothing happened. My product was out there in the realm of all the other products. There were so many products that were selling well on ClickBank—then why wasn't mine?

One day I woke up and saw a FLOOD of ClickBank sales notifications in my inbox and I was shocked. Had I discovered the Holy Grail? Had customers loved my product so much it had gone viral?

Not really.

Doing some research, I found ONE person who had discovered my product and liked it so much he emailed his entire list and got me about 100 sales in one day.

And he made 75 percent commission on every

sale. I had made some money, but he took a large chunk of it. I had to work for 12 hours a day for weeks to launch this product, and this guy simply wrote an email and made more money than I did.

That got me thinking.

That's when I started realizing the power of owning an email list.

The joy of that realization slowly faded away because I had to prepare for my MBA entrance examinations. It was the next logical step for everyone in my college and I couldn't be the only one left behind.

You could say I succumbed to family pressure, but I enjoyed preparing for those exams and answering papers.

As luck would have it, I scored brilliantly on most of these exams and I had interview calls from several top MBA institutes in the country.

However, that was also the time where I had to make a decision.

Our choices define our destiny. No one can take that away from you. Your choice.

And I chose to work on my online business rather than spend the next two years studying finance and marketing at an MBA college.

I had a heart-to-heart with my dad and told

him that even if I failed at this venture—the blame would be on ME. He was neutral about it, having spent his entire life in the academic field of medical science. He couldn't understand at that point why I was rejecting my job offers and interview offers. But I'm grateful that he let me be.

Family drama was over. It was time to hustle and prove to myself and the world I had made the right decision.

I decorated the first floor of my parents' house with orange flooring, orange curtains, orange paint on the cupboards, and an orange sofa. Don't ask me why. I still don't know the reason for choosing an orange palette.

I bought a new Dell computer and a new desk. This one had drawers.

I used to wake up in the morning, walk two steps to sit down at my desk, work till the wee hours of the night, and sleep off.

The hustle had begun.

MY COMPANY

DURING THE NEXT year or so, I experimented with A LOT of affiliate marketing strategies because the entire concept was quite intriguing. All I had to do was find ways to drive traffic to an affiliate offer and make sure I was ROI-positive.

All the while, I started learning about Email Marketing.

With every landing page I put out, I would have an opt-in form.

With every PPC campaign I launched, I would also email my small list about it.

I experimented with every traffic source out there. The more I played around, the more I realised one thing.

All the other traffic sources depended on ROI. I had to pay for traffic and the day I stopped paying, I would stop getting traffic.

But email traffic was different. Sure, I had to spend money to build my list and I was slowly learning how to improve my conversion rates. But once I had that email list, I could send them an email every day and all the traffic I drove from those emails wouldn't put a scratch in my pocket.

It was like: Free Traffic on Demand.

I had quadrupled my revenue from my freelancing days and things were looking up. However, I knew I was capable of doing more.

I had to make it official. Things were getting to a point where I couldn't write:

Copyright, Ritoban Chakrabarti. All rights reserved.

I needed a company. Opening a company in India isn't that easy. However I found an agent who helped me through the entire process.

Now I could write:

Copyright, MarkAce Marketing Pvt. Ltd. All rights reserved.

As fate would have it, I had reached a stage where I was making five figures a month working solo —still with that ridiculously slow internet.

I knew I could go bigger.

I started looking for office space in Chandigarh. Eyebrows were raised wherever I went because no one took a 21-year-old seriously. But after a few meetings, one real estate agent was so impressed with my story, he recommended me to a friend of his who had a newly built plug-and-play IT office infrastructure.

I took that office space and decorated it nicely. I was quite impressed with how Google built their offices. So I set up a pool table, table tennis table, a chill out room, and spaced out the workstations so my staff could work in their own space.

The next step was hiring people.

I thought if I hired twenty other people to do the same thing I was doing—I would make twenty times the money.

Did I? Not really.

In fact, the expenses started to pile up and my burn rate increased to such levels that if I didn't do something differently, I would have to close shop within six months.

That's when I started talking with one of the top internet marketers in the world—Anik Singal.

You'll find his story in Part Three of this book.

He showed me how to leverage the power of email marketing to an extent I had never imagined before. He was talking out of experience, of course, because he had built email lists of hundreds of thousands of people by then.

My plan was launching my own product and doing it RIGHT this time. Getting the marketing right. Capturing email addresses wherever possible.

Getting some solid Joint Venture partners to promote the living bloopers out of my product.

I learnt the concept of 'pre-launch', which is one of the most cost-effective ways to build a list. So if you have a product launch, and you've got several JVs on board, then it's crucial to do a proper pre-launch.

I had created an AWESOME training course called 'Profit Instruments'. It was about an affiliate marketing strategy that involved making small websites that took very little time to set up and got ranked high up in the search engines for product name keywords.

I created three training videos, professional level stuff that I gave away for free during my pre-launch. Those videos taught the entire Profit Instruments strategy in brief. I also revealed a case study of one of my best affiliate websites. People loved it. A lot of JVs promoted the pre-launch opt-in page and drove more than 40,000 leads in less than a week.

Those leads got access to all those training videos for free just for entering their email address—and when the actual product was launched, a lot of those people bought it.

Even though the product was available only for a week—it turned out to be a million dollar launch.

That launch showed me the true power of

owning an email list. If I didn't have those 40,000 leads, I would have had no audience interested in me or my strategies.

After that launch, I started promoting other people's products as an affiliate. I drove a lot of sales for a lot of people and got on a lot of launch leaderboards.

This list also paved the way for my next couple of launches—CPA Instruments and Income Instruments. And because I had promoted other people's products, all of those people signed up to promote my future launches.

It literally was a snowball effect and when I look back how that year played out—it was pure magic.

Let's also take my Email Instruments launch for example. I'm writing this entire book that will be given away for free (the PDF version) after people opt-in. I will have several JVs who will promote that opt-in page and drive leads. And then my goal will be to give those leads massive content (like this book and a couple of videos) leading up to the Email Instruments launch.

So you opted in to receive this book. You're now a part of my email list and it will be a great learning experience for you to see the kind of emails I send out in the coming days. Learn from those emails. Look at the subject lines and the email content. That's how I learnt email copywriting myself.

BUILDING CLICKONOMY

ANIK AND I worked on a lot of projects in the coming years and, in 2014, we had realized one important problem in the email marketing industry.

Now, Anik had already done a big launch that year and his product was about email marketing. He had taught more than 10,000 people with that product. We stopped and looked at what was stopping those people from creating a long-term business with email marketing.

What is the FIRST thing in ANY online business funnel?

What is the BLOODLINE of any online business?

Traffic.

Even though our students were able to setup their email marketing funnels properly, they didn't know how to get targeted and qualified traffic to those funnels. BTW, I'll talk more about traffic in Part 2 of this book.

That got us thinking and we decided to change the industry.

Email advertising (or 'solo ads' or 'email media') was a proven and time-tested way to drive traffic to opt-in pages.

But there was no solid marketplace that could connect both buyers and sellers.

So I put my programming hat on, and worked for more than 400 hours to create the alpha version of Clickonomy in June 2014.

Clickonomy is an email advertising marketplace that lists sellers with neat profiles and reviews so a buyer is sure they are purchasing clicks from the right seller. Clickonomy also handles the entire transaction process and every purchase creates a click project between the buyer and seller where they can communicate easily. Clickonomy also tracks clicks, lets you secure your funds, and makes the entire process of buying and selling clicks as easy as possible. I'm really proud of what we're doing with Clickonomy and how we are making it better every single day.

My main goals were:

- A smooth and sexy interface for buyer and seller communication.

- An easy to use platform which was transparent in every way.

- A place where buyers could LEARN from

sellers and vice versa.

- Buyer security. I created a WALLET system that would store buyer funds securely. And if the buyer is satisfied with the ad buy, then he/she can transfer the funds to the seller.

- Seller security. I created a contract system, along with several fraud detection algorithms, to make sure the buyer funds were coming from legal, non-stolen credit cards.

We had contacts in the industry, so we got a lot of email ad sellers on board. And, of course, when our students heard about the marketplace, they rushed to get in.

Since then we have grown slowly but surely in every way. We are adding more security, ease of use, and cool features every single day.

As of now, Clickonomy has been responsible for more than 600,000 clicks in successfully completed projects.

We have almost 7,000 members and growing fast.

Every day, more and more people get to experience email advertising the Clickonomy way. Check it out: https://www.clickonomy.com

MY LIFESTYLE

SO WHAT IS the Email Lifestyle? If you're thinking fancy cars, nice hotels, expensive watches, then you're not *completely* wrong.

But when I say 'Lifestyle', I mean 'Freedom'.

Freedom from financial worries.

Freedom from health and family issues.

Freedom from a 9 to 5 job.

Time Freedom is a luxury that's much, much more valuable to me than a Ferrari.

And it's not just me. You will read about other successful email marketers in Part 3 of this book and what the Email Lifestyle means to them.

You see, I have the freedom to follow my passions.

I love music and just recorded my first song.

I wrote my first novel a few months ago and I'm back with this book now.

I love travelling. I have travelled to more than a dozen countries in the last few years. I've stayed at the best hotels and resorts without thinking twice.

The Email Lifestyle is the luxury of waking up

when you want to, working on your own time, not having to answer to anybody, having plenty of time in your hands to spend with family and friends, travelling to awesome places, meeting a ton of cool people, and following your dreams and passions.

In fact, the money generated with Email Marketing becomes a FUEL to fulfil your passions. I use my money to invest in the marketing of my book, or to hire a crew to direct my next music video.

Email Marketing is a business that only takes a couple of hours every single day. And you have the rest of the day to yourself. You can do your business while chilling at the beach with your wife.

The best part is ANYONE can do this. And I will show you how.

Heck, I got started on an old computer sitting on a little desk in my parents' house in India with ridiculously slow internet, while dealing with college pressure and family expectations.

So, what's your excuse?

PART TWO

The Lessons

10,000 FOOT OVERVIEW

WHILE THERE ARE a lot of ways to approach Email Marketing, I will be talking from the *newbie* perspective. Even if you are an experienced email marketer, you'll be able to pick up a lot of nuggets from the following chapters and directly plug them in your current business. But if you're new to this, pay close attention because we will explore the possibilities of Email Marketing with a strategic step-by-step approach.

My approach will be to NOT confuse you with a thousand technicalities. You can implement so many customizations to your funnels if you're good at programming/designing or know someone who is. My goal is to be beginner-friendly and exploit the arsenal of awesome web-based tools that are at your disposal. They automate 95 percent of the process so you can focus more on scaling and improving your business.

My second goal will be exposing you to the simple concepts that can help you set up a long term, profitable Email Marketing business. A LOT of people are making six and seven figures just using the power of Email Marketing and I hope you join that club really soon.

However, this is NOT a 'get rich quick' scheme and should not be treated as such. The covenants of Email Marketing are sound and sacred. I want you to treat this business like you would any other. It requires blood, sweat, and tears. It requires you to be patient and keep hustling—as ANY other business would.

This is NOT a 'push button' solution to making millions. I say this because I don't believe such solutions exist and, even if they do, they are not long-term ones. If you're interested in quitting your day job and becoming financially free, Email Marketing will pave the way for you. But you need to WORK for it. You need to push a lot of buttons, chase down a lot of people, stay up late at night typing away at that keyboard, and be religious about emailing your list regularly.

Being consistent with emailing your list is one of the core factors that will determine your success right from the beginning. I know a lot of people feel discouraged when they have small email lists and don't email regularly because they know they will not get a considerable number of clicks. That's a perfectly fine mindset if you want to fail. But if you want to succeed, you need to create a HABIT of emailing your list at least five times a week. Write an email every day, right from the beginning.

I'm a big fan of the step-by-step approach. I have taught more than 25,000 people and my students have seen the BEST results when they approach a strategy step-by-step. And that's exactly how I plan to teach you. I will lay down the foundation, throw the bricks in place, solidify them with cement, and cover it up with a roof. I will give you all the information you'll need to start running.

You need to IMPLEMENT what I teach. It's the only thing I ask you to do. Implement. Execute. Hustle. Don't just read for the sake of reading. This is not a story book. This is real life. I'm handing you a complete blueprint that can put rockets to your income and give you a stable long-term business. So it's completely fair for me to ask you to implement.

I call this the 'Email Instruments' strategy.

Email Instruments is a **long-term business.** It does not mean you have to work twenty hours a day for five years to get results out of this business. But what I'm trying to tell you is, if you put in the hard work in the initial days, the amount of work you'll need to do in the future to sustain this business will be quite less and the revenue will increase over time.

We will be setting up **long-term funnels.** A long-term funnel is something that gives you consistent revenue over a long period of time. Let's compare that with the service industry. Let's just say you charge $20 an hour freelancing and working for clients doing programming or designing or handling customer support or whatever expertise you have.

Even if you charge $20 an hour, the amount of money you make at the end of the day will based upon the number of hours you put in that very day. If you stop working the next day, you will stop making money.

I'm a big fan of automation.

An Email Instruments business can never be 100 percent automated, because even if you have the funnels set right that add new subscribers to your list on autopilot, you still have to be religious about emailing your list regularly. But it's MUCH better than having to slave away for hours working to build someone else's dream while your dream languishes in the shadows. If you follow everything to a T, you'll notice how easy it is to automate most of the elements of your funnels.

I'll teach you how to **convert your passions into a business.** I love writing, and in my first launch – Profit Instruments, I wrote a nice report that everybody liked and I just published my first novel.

This is my second published book and, if you look closely, you'll observe how I tied this in with my Email Marketing business. Almost certainly, you opted-in to my email list to receive this book. If you haven't already, I hope you do because there's A LOT you can learn from my experience. I don't shy away from sharing every part of my business with my list.

Back to the point—I'm writing to help take my business to the next level. If you're passionate about golf, I'll teach you how to convert that to an Email Instruments business. Music? Will do! Painting? Of course! Cars? For sure! You get the point. If you have a passion and there's a market for it—then you can create a long-term Email Instruments business out of it.

That's exactly why I love this model. When you are working on your passions, it feels as though you're not working at all. It becomes a part of you and you actually ENJOY putting in those long hours. The hustle seems so much sweeter at the end of the day because you will be able to impact the lives of so many like-minded people with your emails.

We also will learn how to create an **evergrowing email list**. While I cannot guarantee what your growth curve will look like, I can almost certainly say it will have an upward curve. The beauty of this model is your list grows with you. The more you grow, the more influential you become, and that's how even more people subscribe to your list. It works like magic. All you need is dedication and discipline. The rest will take care of itself.

How to **build a relationship with your email list.** Relationships are key when it comes to anything related to business. Let's just say you're married. It's important to have a nice, healthy relationship with your wife. If you have kids, it's important to have a distinct relationship with your kids so they respect you, adore you, and listen to you.

Relationships are important everywhere and it's the same with your email list. Don't just treat your email list like a number. A lot of people say, "Okay, I've got 30,000 people in my email list." That's just a number. You don't need to focus on the number as much as you need to focus on how you're treating those people. These are real people who are getting your emails.

If you want to be seen as an authority in a niche, you have to interact with your list regularly and with your own voice. You want to leave a legacy? Be good to your list and those people will remember you for it. They will spread the word and become your evangelists. That's the dream, and you are only moments from getting that realised.

Let's dive in and see the steps involved in setting up an effective Email Instruments business.

The Email Instruments Funnel

You drive TRAFFIC to an OPT-IN PAGE. Once a person enters their email address on the opt-in page, they are taken to a POP. If they don't opt-in, and try to go back or try to close the browser, present them an EXIT OPT-IN PAGE. In the backend, every email address entered in your opt-in page is stored in an EMAIL LIST DATABASE. You can send emails to that database in the form of AUTORESPONDERS AND NEWSLETTERS. On your POP as well as in your emails, you will be promoting either your own products or AFFILIATE OFFERS in your niche.

Once you understand each aspect of the funnel, then the flow won't seem confusing. In fact, learn to embrace it right now. This is where the fun begins.

The EI Funnel has seven parts:

Traffic - It's the lifeblood of any online business. You need people to enter your funnel.

Opt-In Page - This is where most of the action will happen. This is where a portion of your traffic will become a part of your email list.

POP – 95 percent of marketers don't use this correctly and lose out on a lot of money. You won't have to. It's also called the 'Post Opt-In Page'.

Exit Opt-In Page - Takes less than half an hour to integrate, but increases your overall conversion rate by up to 30 percent.

Email List Database - This is where all your subscribers will be stored. Some amazing systems out there let you manage your email database inexpensively.

Autoresponders and Newsletters - These are two types of emails that will go out to your subscribers.

Affiliate Offers - If you have your own product, well and good. If not, promote other people's products and make money as an affiliate.

Overwhelming? Fret not, my friend. For, if you keep reading this book for another hour, you will have a much deeper understanding of the entire funnel.

SELECTING A NICHE

THE FIRST STEP of the process is having an honest reflection.

What's the one thing that makes you tick and even if you spend hours studying, analysing, and working on that one thing—you'll never get tired of it?

In other words—What's your PASSION?

Not all your passions will be profitable and you shouldn't start putting in all the hard work in a niche that has little to no chance of yielding a profit.

If you have no ideas yet, don't worry because I'll be handing over a list of some proven hot niches which you can jump into right away.

But let's focus on the niche selection process first.

Fortunately, there's a checklist you can follow that will determine whether a niche is profitable or not.

- Does your niche have a lot of products that are selling well?
- Does your niche have a lot of buyers?

- Will you be able to market to this niche effectively?

- Are YOU interested in the niche?

You need to find the answers to these four questions. The easiest way to start is by making a list of all the things you are passionate about. Don't think. Just write them down.

How often do you have an awesome idea or a thought and you think about it for a while and then get lost in the daily grind? Do you think you remember that awesome idea you had a couple of years ago? In most certainty, you don't.

Why? Because you didn't write it down.

It's extremely important to write stuff down. And I don't use a cool web application to take notes. I have my handy pen and paper—the oldest tools in the business.

So write down the list of things you're interested in.

Once you have that list ready, then it will be time to start the 'Niche Research' process.

Does your niche have a lot of products that are selling well?

To answer this question, you can go to these three places:

- ClickBank.com

- OfferVault.com
- Magazines.com

Let's talk about ClickBank first, because if you're interested in selling digital products online, ClickBank has the largest collection of digital products in several niches.

Step 1: Head over to the ClickBank Marketplace.

Step 2: To get niche ideas, have a look at all of ClickBank's categories of products. They have sub-categorized niches into sub-niches as well. It's a great way to understand what niches are out there.

Step 3: Select a category and then look at the top-selling products. With each product listing, you will see a 'gravity' number. The higher the gravity, the better. Gravity is determined by the number of affiliates who have sold that particular product recently. So this number answers two of your questions. If the gravity is high, it means the product is marketable and buyers are out there.

Step 4: If you see three or more products in a category with a gravity of more than 30—then it's a HOT niche. Because that means there are multiple products in that niche that are selling well. So, if you were to launch a product in that niche, you KNOW you would be able to take a slice of the market share.

OfferVault is basically a marketplace for CPA offers. CPA offers pay out affiliates per lead. It's the short form of 'Cost Per Action' or 'Cost Per Acquisition'. OfferVault has a huge directory of CPA offers in multiple networks in a lot of niches. It's a great place to get ideas for niches and products that you potentially can promote as an affiliate. The only catch before jumping into a niche is you need to apply to a CPA network first. Once you get in a network, then you get options to promote multiple offers in their network.

Magazines.com is yet another place to get brilliant niche ideas. Simply head over to their 'Best Sellers' section and you'll see a list of magazines that sell well. Some of these will be the common ones, but you'll find some magazines in unorthodox niches as well.

Hot and Proven Niches

Since I've been doing this a long time, I have a handy dandy list of niches that I know, for a fact, are profitable.

And since you've made it this far into the book, its time I gave you that list right now.

Internet Marketing - This always will be one of the most important industries because it's extremely profitable. There are a lot of products, a lot of marketplaces, a lot of buyers, and it's really easy to get your foot in the door in this niche.

Personal Development - It's also called PD in the inner circles. It deals with meditation, motivation, affirmations, law of attraction, and how to be successful, among other things. You can create your own products or software in this niche or promote others' products as an affiliate because there are hundreds of high-converting offers. It's got a lot of buyers. Everybody wants to be motivated, know about how to attract wealth and prosperity and happiness in their lives.

Weight Loss - Everybody wants to have a nice figure or a nice body and look good, and there are so many people who are overweight and want to lose that excess fat. Again, a ton of products to promote as an affiliate. You can create your own weight loss guide and sell it.

Recipes and Cooking – This niche has a lot of different sub-niches. For example, the Paleo Diet and the Lemonade Diet. This is a winning combination because everybody eats food and a lot of people want to know about the latest dieting system out there.

Property - Everybody wants a property of their own. There are a lot of different guides, videos, memberships, forums and a lot of different things on real estate where people are willing to spend money.

Electronics: Even though this has a lot of physical products, you can be an affiliate. For example, you are an expert in iPads and you know the insider tips and tricks on iPads, so you can probably get inside the iPad niche. Because there are so many buyers, so many products, there's just so many different kind of things related to iPads.

Investing and Trading - This is more about Forex and personal finance. Forex is basically foreign exchange and personal finance deals with binary options and day trading. You can create products on how to trade. So if you're interested in this niche, you definitely can try it out because a lot of people want to learn how to invest. A lot of people want to learn how to get inside the share market.

Pets - You've got dogs, cats, hamsters, spiders. Each type of pet becomes a niche and each pet has multiple subniches. For example, dogs have hot sub-niches such as dog training, dog maintenance, dog grooming, dog food, and the list goes on.

Apart from these, check out some other niches that are proven to be profitable.

- Relationship advice
- Education
- Jobs

- Acne
- Reiki
- Panic attacks
- Divorce and dating
- Quit smoking
- Yoga

The reason I'm giving you all these niches on a silver platter is to help you see the possibilities out there. Each of the niches I've mentioned above can become a million dollar business for you. The power is in your hands.

So choose a niche you are interested in and go for it.

AUTORESPONDER ACCOUNT

AN AUTORESPONDER ACCOUNT is the first thing you'll need to set up your Email Marketing business.

With the advancements in marketing technology, we now have access to an inordinate amount of automation with list building. Leading from the front are autoresponder companies that let you store email addresses in databases, let you email them based on several customized parameters, let you split test and track clicks, let you segment and scrub your list for effective results, and provide an easy click-click interface for managing everything.

You can sign up for several companies (most offer a free trial) including, but not limited to, GetResponse, AWeber, MailChimp, and SendLane. SendLane is the latest offering created by my close friend Jimmy Kim. He has shared his story, which you can read in Part Three of this book.

All of these companies primarily fulfil the basic function of storing email addresses for your lists and providing a slick web-based interface for emailing your lists. You pay a monthly fee to these companies based on the SaaS model and get to use their technology.

If you don't have an autoresponder account, I highly recommend you get one. There are software programs out there you can install on your server for a nominal one-time payment. I have tried them and don't recommend them if you're starting out.

Email deliverability is a major factor in our business. The reputable companies I've mentioned above have a bunch of tried and tested IPs in their arsenal and have more than 99 percent email deliverability. That's where the "own sever" autoresponder account fails. Unless you have the technology in place to host multiple IP addresses whitelisted by email providers, your deliverability will suffer. That, in turn, will be a lost cause for your Email Marketing business.

Without getting all technical, simply signup with one of the companies I mentioned above. They are all reasonably priced.

FREE GIVEAWAY

IT'S TIME TO start building your Email Instrument, and the first step is creating your free giveaway. In an opt-in page, you need to entice people to give their email address. Why would a person give you their email address?

You need to give them something in return. Think of it like a barter system.

You give them something for free in exchange for their email address.

It needs to be something that they would value. Something that they would WANT to have.

It's always beneficial to have a nice, valuable giveaway because, in the end, if a person gives you their email address and is happy with the giveaway, then they'll be a loyal subscriber.

It's important to give them something awesome right from the get-go because this is your entry point.

Relevance is very important because, let's say you're in the golfing niche, and the back-end product you have is related to improving your golf swing.

The free giveaway ideally should be something

like a free report on 'Ten Ways to Improve Your Golf Swing in a Week'.

It also should be personalized.

If your giveaway doesn't have a personality of its own, let's say you just copied and pasted somebody else's work, or you just take some articles from somewhere and compile them into a report and then give it to your subscribers—that's not ideal at all.

This will be the first time your subscriber is interacting with you, and they get to know YOU. Get inside their minds and tell them you are somebody they should follow, respect and listen to.

The point of the entire Email Instruments process is building a funnel. It can be an affiliate funnel. It also could be your funnel, if you have your own products. The important part here is the giveaway should BUILD up your funnel.

For example, I had an opt-in page where I was giving away a free report on how I made $1,409 and generated some 600 subscribers in three days.

Once a person opted-in, they were taken to a blog where they could download the free report. The free report also pre-sold the affiliate offer I was promoting.

Inside the free report and inside that blog, we had banners for the affiliate offer I was promoting.

Once a person actually read through the entire report, they were enticed to click my affiliate link.

You must be thinking it'll be difficult to set-up a free giveaway. Not really, because there are multiple ways to create a free giveaway of your own. You can actually create a giveaway in mere minutes.

There are different types of giveaways:

Free Report (PDF)

A free report is basically a PDF file, or it could also be a nice big article on your blog. This is the easiest to set up because you can fire up your word processor and write down a couple thousand words about something interesting in your niche.

Free Video

With the advancements in technologies and webcams, it has become really easy to shoot videos. If you're one of those people who is shy in front of the camera and don't want to show your face, you can actually record your screen as well using software such as ScreenFlow or Camtasia.

The best part is, the video doesn't even need to be yours. On your opt-in page, you could say, "Free video reveals ten ways to improve your golf swing." Once the person opts in, you can take them through your affiliate link to a golf product sales video.

Free Infographic

Infographics are sophisticated images that contain a lot of stats and graphs, and a lot of interesting and cool data about a topic. Comics are also quite catchy and they convey information in a creative way.

They can be consumed quite easily, and people actually appreciate you giving them not just words on paper, but actually something they can see and visualize. You can pull it off if you're good with graphic designing or know someone who is.

Free Audio/Podcast

I remember on one of my Email Instruments, I was giving away a free audio series on meditation. I had these meditation sound clips, so I just uploaded them to SoundCloud.com and then embedded them in my blog.

I actually received quite a lot of comments from people thanking me for those meditation audios.

You can outsource the creation of your giveaway on sites such as Elance.com or Freelancer.com.

The easiest way to create a free report is going to iWriter.com because they have people who have written articles for years.

If somebody has good reviews, then hire them and they'll write an article for you for a fixed fee. It's quite inexpensive and you own the copyright to the content.

Let's say you're creating a 3,000 word report. You could hire three writers to write down different sections of the report and then combine all of them.

Now, you can get creative with the giveaway creation process in a lot of ways, but the fastest way to get started is using PLR content. PLR means Private Label Rights.

There are places where you can get cool private label rights products. You simply take a product, modify it to your liking, add your name—and voila! You have a free giveaway.

My favourite website for sourcing PLR products is PLRAssassin.com because they have a huge collection—I think more than 8,000 PLR products in all sorts of niches. You can get some good giveaway ideas for creating reports just by looking at the free products listed on PLRAssassin.

The key here is remembering not all products carry the same licenses. It's important to check the license you get for the product.

There's MRR—which means Master Resell Rights. You also have Personal Rights products. There's RR—which means Resell Rights.

Whenever you download a product from

PLRAssassin, it will carry a license.pdf file or license.txt file. Just check out that license file and see what you're allowed to do.

It'll mention if you're allowed to give it away to your list. Or if you're allowed to modify the content.

Don't just copy and paste. Give it a twist and make it your own.

OPTIN PAGES

AN OPT-IN FORM is the gateway to your Email Instruments funnel. It's the first thing a visitor sees when they land on your opt-in page. The goal of the opt-in page is to have the highest possible conversion rate.

If you have a niche blog, then you should have an opt-in form on your blog sidebar—without fail. Nowadays, there's technology that lets you setup neat opt-in forms anywhere on any website you own. I'll recommend one such tool at the end of this chapter that I use personally.

You can have several fields in an opt-in form, but the most important field is, of course, email address.

In most cases, having just an email address field will do.

You can also choose to add more fields, such as name, phone number, address, country, etc.

You have to remember that your conversion rate will drop if you have more fields. That's why I recommend sticking with just an email address field because that's all you need to communicate with your subscribers.

Every niche is different and conversion rates of different opt-in pages in different niches vary greatly. What you should be most concerned about is how you monetize your list—both with autoresponders as well as POP.

I've created opt-in pages that generated over 70 percent conversion rate. That means if 100 people landed on my opt-in page, 70 of them would give me their email address. That's huge!

You might not get such conversion rates in the first go because a lot of factors determine your conversion rate.

An opt-in page has four important elements:

Headline

Short, crisp, and hard hitting. The headline is very important as it lies at the top of your opt-in page. Typically in a large, bold font, the headline conveys what you're giving away and it conveys that with style and panache. It can be something like, "Unlock the Power of Your Mind in 5 Days with 5 FREE Guided Meditations". The opt-in page with this headline converted at more than 60 percent. Take a look at the Email Instruments opt-in page and other places where YOU opted in. If that headline worked for you, then it will work for others, too. The next time you land at an opt-in page, look at the headline and try visualizing how you could make it better.

Opt-in Form

As I mentioned earlier, you should aim to have the least number of fields in your opt-in form. Apart from the fields, the submit button is the next crucial element of an opt-in page. It needs to be big, bold, and the colour of the button should be yellow or orange or green. These colours, when used against a nice contrasting backdrop, create the ultimate opt-in page. The text on the submit button should be something like: Click Here For FREE Instant Access.

Images

This is the tricky part because it's been proven that a nice, relevant giveaway image or background image helps increase conversions drastically. However, if the image you choose is poor, overused, or not highly relevant then it can bring DOWN your conversion rates as well. You won't need a striking background image on all opt-in pages. If the opt-in page design is such that there's a lot of empty space in the background—then I highly recommend setting up a background image that conveys the message of your giveaway. For example, if your giveaway is about losing weight, then your background image can be a weighing scale, or a man/woman with a measuring tape around their belly, or a fit man/woman running... You get the point. If you have a nice image of the giveaway, like an e-book cover, or a video screenshot, and it blends in well with your opt-in page —only then do I suggest you use it.

Sub-Headline/Bullets

Some opt-in page designs have bullet points and sub headlines. Even though they are not required on an opt-in page, if the bullet points are able to convey the awesomeness of your giveaway—then go for it. Same with the sub-headline. A standard sub-headline (text written in a smaller font than the headline and placed right below the headline) is something like, "Enter your email address below to get the free report."

Several web-based tools out there let you create stunning opt-in pages in minutes without having to touch a single line of code. The most popular one among email marketers is LeadPages.

LeadPages has more than 100 high-converting templates that you can customize heavily using a slick web-based interface. Then you can split-test multiple pages as well as publish them any way you want. WordPress, HTML, Facebook Tabs—they give you a lot of easy publishing options as well as some cool conversion stats and reports.

I use LeadPages for creating a lot of my own opt-in pages. If you're starting out, I highly recommend you use their service. You get exceptional value for the price they charge.

POP

WHAT HAPPENS WHEN visitors hit submit on your opt-in page? They get taken to another page, which I call the Post Opt-in Page or POP.

In popular terminology, it's also referred to as the ThankYou Page.

I'll stick with POP.

Doesn't matter what you call it. What matters is how you're monetizing that page.

The #1 mistake most marketers make with an Email Marketing funnel is they don't optimize the POP.

I think it's all in the mindset.

When someone looks at your opt-in page and decides to give you their email address—it means they are interested in what you have to say. You have their attention.

It's an utter waste to let their attention dwindle by showing them a simple 'Thank You' message. You are literally doing a disservice by not showing your new leads something fresh and interesting they would love to see.

It can be your free giveaway, or an affiliate offer, or just a banner promoting an affiliate offer.

It's extremely important to monetize that page because that's where you will start recovering your investment in traffic. If your POP is set up the right way, you will start generating revenue with your list from day one.

I know people who recover 100 percent of their cost in acquiring traffic right on the POP. That means the revenue generated with their list will be ALL profit.

There are three types of POP:

Redirector POP

This is a simple page that shows a thank you message with a countdown of seven seconds that redirects the end-user to an affiliate offer or the sales page of a product you own. It's effective because you can deliver the giveaway via the first autoresponder message while promoting an offer straight up.

Blog POP

For long term funnels, I prefer the Blog POP because it's not just a simple one page—but a complete blog that's set up with multiple monetization plugins. You can easily deliver any sort of content on a simple WordPress blog and add banners on the sidebar, at the footer of each post, as well as a Hello Bar at the top of every page promoting an affiliate offer.

Info POP

Several templates are available on the LeadPages platform that let you create simple Info POPs. The main elements of that page are a thank you message along with a banner promoting an affiliate offer or a video pre-selling an affiliate offer or your own product with a button to buy that product below the video. You can also place your social buttons (FB, Twitter, G+) towards the bottom of the page.

We have created a very simple tool that lets you create the Redirector POP within seconds. You can find it here: http://imconversion.com/popgenerator/

Installing and setting up a WordPress blog for the Blog POP is also quite simple and doesn't take much time. If you want to create long-term funnels and are serious about your business—it's imperative you learn how to use WordPress because there's so much you can do with it. So much.

Take the POP seriously and it will go a LONG way in taking your Email Instruments funnel to the next level.

SENDING EMAIL

WHEN A PERSON subscribes to your email list, they are automatically added to the email database I told you about. If you have a specific set of autoresponders set up in your autoresponder account, then they will start receiving those messages.

Autoresponders

Autoresponders are basically automatic emails that go out to your email database whenever a parameter you have set in your account gets matched.

You can set up timed autoresponders (which are the most common), which means the system will send out emails to your subscribers based on the time they joined your list. One goes out instantly (Day 0), and you can set up emails to go out on Day 2, Day 4, and so on.

You can set up several types of autoresponder parameters. You can setup if-then conditions like: If they click on Email A, then send them Email B after one day.

Autoresponders have become an intricate part of every email marketer's business because these are pre-set emails that are sent automatically.

Automation is one of the keys to a successful email marketing business. If you have, say, 30 emails pre-set to go out during the two months after a subscriber joins your list—then it's completely hands off for you.

Newsletters

What do you do when you find out about a brand new product you want to promote to your entire list? Or if you're launching your own product and want your entire list to know about it? Or if you've written a blog post and want everyone to know about it?

That's when newsletters come handy. In their nascent form, newsletters are email blasts to your entire list. You can write an email, select which emails lists you want the email sent to, and then schedule the email to be sent at a specific date and time, or have it sent instantly.

Nowadays, you can schedule your newsletters to go out at a specific time, keeping in mind the time zone difference. So if you have a newsletter scheduled to be sent at 8 a.m. tomorrow, then your Indian subscribers will get it when its 8 a.m. Indian Standard Time, and U.S. subscribers will get it when its 8 a.m. there. Pretty sweet.

The key to a successful email marketing business is emailing regularly.

You should have at least 7-8 autoresponders set out to go to your subscribers over the course of two weeks. The first autoresponder email that goes out instantly after a person opts in should introduce who you are and what value the person will gain from being on your list, and a link to your free giveaway.

You should send out newsletters AT LEAST every other day. I recommend emailing your list every day of the week except Saturday and Sunday. So that's five emails per week.

Sending email should become a part of your daily routine. It's like how you take a shower every day. So you should send an email every day too.

Mix and match information emails with product promotions. Don't just send information emails every day. Don't feel shy about sending promotional emails. Promote affiliate offers. Promote your products. Promote email advertising clicks. You need to send at least two promo emails every week.

It will get boring at times. You will not be motivated to write an email every day if your list is small—but don't let that bother you.

Leverage the power of autoresponders and newsletters. Your list is your audience and you owe it to them to reach out and communicate. They are a part of your list for a reason. Your voice will now be heard.

GETTING TRAFFIC

NOT ALL TRAFFIC is equal. There are hundreds of ways to drive traffic to your opt-in page, and I've tried almost all of them. Over the years I've discovered two important factors that will determine your ROI and conversion rates.

Targeted Traffic

If you drive people interested in pet grooming to a golf swing opt-in page, then you're really doing them and yourself a disservice. The greater your targeting with traffic, the better results you'll get. So when a person searches for 'I want to groom my dog' in Google and you have a sponsored Google ad that goes to a dog grooming opt-in page, that's as targeted as it gets. But the question is, how do you find a monster traffic source that can drive consistent targeted traffic to your opt-in pages?

Qualified Traffic

Let's say you have a Facebook page about dog grooming with a lot of fans and you publish a video in there telling them about '5 Magnificent Dog Grooming Tips' and then tell them to go to a link (which is basically your opt-in page) where you reveal 15 more unique dog grooming tips. Do you think the people who see the video and then go to your opt-in page, won't give you their email address? That's what qualified means. The more you qualify a visitor before they land on your opt-in page, the higher your conversion rate will be.

If you're able to drive both targeted AND qualified traffic to your opt-in page, then you'll get the best conversion rates possible with a higher ROI opportunity.

There are several ways to drive traffic:
- Facebook Ads
- Google AdWords
- SEO
- PPV
- Media Buys
- Social Media
... The list goes on.

My goal is to NOT confuse you with a hundred traffic sources. Enough has been said about all of them already.

The best traffic source for both targeted and qualified traffic, especially for building an email list is Email Advertising. Also called 'solo ads' or 'email media'.

Let me tell you how email advertising works. Let's say there's this guy, John, who has an email list of 20,000 people in the WEIGHT LOSS niche with whom he's built a great relationship over the years.

When John sends an email to his list, he gets 1,000-plus people to respond to it. Every single time. And let's say you asked him to promote YOUR weight loss opt-in page. So he sends an email pre-selling your opt-in page to his entire list.

So the people clicking the link in John's email land on your opt-in page and become a part of YOUR email list. That's as targeted and qualified as it gets.

But the question is, where do you find people like John? Don't worry my friend—for I have built an entire marketplace full of sellers willing to sell high quality clicks to you.

Remember Clickonomy?

That's the reason we built Clickonomy in the first place, create a one-stop solution for buyers and sellers willing to engage in email advertising. Help first-timers get complete and transparent access to a huge traffic source where they can control how much they spend and who they buy clicks from.

Leverage the power of Clickonomy to drive traffic to your opt-in pages.

COPYWRITING BASICS

EVEN THOUGH I can't go deeply into copywriting and the psychology behind mind-blowing copy, if you follow the simple rules I've mentioned below, you should be able to create opt-in pages that convert really well.

Copywriting will come in handy in two different aspects. While writing emails, and while writing opt-in page copy.

Email Copywriting

The subject line is the first thing a person sees when they receive an email from you. The ONLY goal of the subject line is to get the person to OPEN your email. I've written subject lines that have had more than 30 percent open rate and I've written subject lines that have had 5 percent open rates. There's no fixed rule on writing subject lines, but the best suggestion I can give you is this: Look at your own inbox. Search for emails you received from other email marketers and then look at the ones you actually opened. Study the subject lines of those emails. What was different? Why did it entice you to open? Once you've looked at 20 or 30 such subject lines from that perspective, you'll start to understand how to write your own subject lines.

The email body copy is an entirely different game all together. There are a few things you need to remember:

- Write short paragraphs. Nothing more than two or three lines.

- Hit a blank space between each paragraph.

- The LINKS in your email need to be highlighted and mentioned separately, not just as an anchor text to some phrase. It should be more on the lines of: ==> Click here to watch the free video

Opt-in Page Copywriting

I cannot stress the importance of the word FREE enough. Mention the word FREE at least 2-3 times in strategic locations in your opt-in page. Mention it both in your headline and your submit button. We have actually split-tested a page which was similar in every way. It was just that one version of the page had no mention of the word FREE and the other had two mentions of it. No surprise as to which one converted better. The FREE version had a 30 percent better conversion rate.

Although not recommended on all opt-in pages, assigning a VALUE to your giveaway on your opt-in page has proven to help increase conversions. So you can mention something like: $47 Value. I've tried this strategy on some of my opt-in pages, but only when the value can be proven. If the giveaway previously has been sold at that price or if you've taken a PLR product which almost always has a retail price, you can mention that price as the value amount on your opt-in page. Please refrain from assigning random value amounts off the top of your head.

Once you start working on your opt-in pages, you will realize the best ones are short, hard hitting, and on point. There's no need to write several paragraphs full of content, and while some opt-in pages read like a long form letter, I don't recommend that. Your headline, opt-in form, and submit button all should be ABOVE THE FOLD. That means a visitor shouldn't have to scroll down the page to view the opt-in form. It should be right there when the page loads.

There's a lot of advanced stuff that's been shared by people who are 10x better than me. A simple Google search on 'email copywriting' and 'opt-in page copywriting' will suffice. Let Google be your friend and guide you. I have laid down the foundation and given you the basic rules. Sticking to these rules will be enough for you to build an awesome opt-in page. However, never stop learning and always strive to improve yourself.

NEXT LEVEL

I CALL MYSELF an experimental marketer and that's because I love playing around with different aspects of marketing.

Over the years, I've partaken in hundreds of experiments in all forms of online marketing. I've learnt from the pros and others have learnt from me and become pros themselves. I wish you the same success and one way to get massive success with your Email Instruments campaigns is by making subtle changes and additions that help increase your opt-in conversion rate and revenue generation several fold.

I cannot stress enough how important the following three points are:

Split Testing

The more you play this game, the more you will realize how important NUMBERS are. Setting up effective funnels is all about mathematics.

X visitors go to an opt-in page. Y number of people become a part of your email list. Z number of people buy the product you recommend on your POP. Sending regular autoresponders and newsletters helps you recover your budget and then you start profiting from your list.

Split testing is about improving Y and Z.

Y is dependent on your opt-in page conversion rate. Always keep improving. Never stop improving. And the best way to improve your conversion rate is split testing multiple versions of your opt-in page and seeing what's converting better. And then improving that page even more.

Complicated you say? Not really, because several tools out there help you carry out these split testing experiments. LeadPages has built-in split testing that works right out of the box. You can create an opt-in page inside LeadPages, and create a different version of that page within minutes.

I recommend you split test four important elements of an opt-in page.

- Design
- Headline
- Signup Button
- Images

The first split test you should run is with two different looking designs of your opt-in page with everything else kept the same. Once you've driven about 1,000 visitors (500 to each version), then you'll have data on which is converting better.

Pick that one and then split test two different versions of your headline with everything else kept the same.

And follow the same process for the submit button (colour and text) and your images.

After you've sent about 5,000 visitors to your split tests, you will know with 100 percent certainty which version is converting the best.

Then use the lessons from those experiments to create your future opt-in pages. That's how you grow and evolve in this industry, my friend.

Exit Opt-in Page

This is something I always use with my Email Instruments funnels. I used to hate exit popups. They are annoying. But you know what else they are? A life saver.

One of my opt-in pages had a conversion rate of 50 percent. I was happy, but I knew I could do better.

So I implemented an exit opt-in page with a different design and different headline like: This Is Your Last Chance, and a different background image.

The results were shocking. The initial opt-in page had the same 50 percent conversion rate, but what happened was my overall conversion rate ended up being 70 percent.

Earlier I was getting 500 subscribers for 1,000 visitors. Now, I was getting 700 subscribers for the same 1,000 people. That's HUGE—considering it was a few minutes of extra work in setting it up.

That's how you take a decent campaign to become a long-term profitable funnel.

LeadPages has the exit popup functionality built in—there's no need for you to write code.

Segmentation, Scrubbing, Analytics

I love GetResponse and use it for most of my email marketing. They have some pretty neat features that make my life a whole lot easier. Once your email list reaches five figures or more, that's when you should start to take these points seriously.

Scrubbing basically means you're removing your inactive subscribers from your list. Let's say you have a list of 10,000 people and you've been emailing regularly to them for two months.

You can go inside GetResponse and add a filter to see how many people have not opened and not clicked on ANY of your emails in the last two months. If a person hasn't opened or clicked a link in any email, then it's time to let them go. You delete those people from your list.

It goes a long way in improving your overall open rate and click rate—and that ensures your email deliverability is top notch.

There are several ways to segment your list. You can create a segment of people who regularly open and click your emails. You can create a segment of people on your list who are from the U.K. and send them U.K.-specific emails. You can create a segment of people who were referred by a specific traffic source (for that to work, you have to pass specific parameters on your opt-in form).

Segmentation comes in handy when you don't want to do a full email blast—but only target a specific set of people.

Almost all autoresponder services show you cool analytics. You can check how many people open and click on your newsletters and autoresponders. You can compare the stats of two emailings side by side and then LEARN why one email had a better open rate. Checking stats is crucial in your learning process. It's the one thing I rely on when I want to improve my email copywriting.

As I told you before, it's a numbers game. When you're looking at reports and analytics—you see proof. You see the actual numbers. Let those numbers teach you what's working and what's not. Never presume anything.

PROFIT RECYCLING

I WAS BRAINSTORMING with my mentor in Singapore a few months ago and we came up with a brilliant email marketing plan. We quickly did some calculations on a piece of paper and it seemed too good to be true. So, being the experimental marketer I am, I decided to try it out. I even gave the plan to my team and they showed it to some of our top students.

It was all hush-hush and we just waited to see the results. We recently compiled the results and it was mind-blowing.

The plan worked. For every single person. So much so we decided to make a full training series on the plan as well as a neat tool on how to execute it. I can hardly contain my excitement. All right, so here's the thing. The concept is simple. It's pure mathematics.

Step 1: You start off with a budget. It can be $500 or $5,000 or $20,000—based on your capacity. I recommend starting off with a budget of at least $500 because that will drive a decent amount of test traffic to your funnel.

Step 2: You create an Email Instruments funnel that's guaranteed to make money from Day ONE. And put in some key elements in the picture that multiply your revenue. Things such as affiliate links in your emails, promoting a new product launch to your list, selling clicks via Email Advertising. All are very easy to execute.

Step 3: You recover your investment within a few days. And RE-INVEST it to get more subscribers to your list. Let's say you make $100 every day for five days. You keep re-investing the $100 for the next five days. So you're not actually putting in more money. You just re-invested the same $500.

Step 4: You keep re-investing the old budget. That keeps building your list exponentially while you keep generating massive revenue from your list that goes directly to your bank account.

I call this the **'Profit Recycling Method'** and I'm so excited you're one of the first people to know about it.

The entire concept relies on the fact that your Email Instruments funnel is heavily monetized for the highest conversion rate right off the bat. You'll need to be very active with your new formed email list when you start your Profit Recycling campaign because your goal is recovering the initial budget.

But make sure whatever money you're making until you recover the budget goes directly to buy more traffic for your funnel.

The key here is in creating a mind-set of budget fixing, sticking to that budget, and re-investing over and over.

We have had students who recovered their initial budget on Day 1 and then re-invested it completely starting on Day 2. They now have a huge list simply by following this strategy. Most of them then increased their budget.

The higher your budget grows, the more subscribers you add to your list with every email ad buy. It's pure magic and your list keep growing every time you re-invest.

We've also built a quick little tool that's called the **'Profit Recycling Manager'**. You get to monitor your budget, expenditures, profit, and take your Email Instruments to the next level. In fact, this tool is something I now use on a daily basis. It lets you enter your budget, how you're spending your money, how you're making your money, your profit margins with every campaign, and the pace at which you're growing your email list. It's a must-have tool and we're making it better every day.

The entire Profit Recycling method, along with

the tool, is only available at emailinstruments.com.

VERY, VERY few people in the industry are doing this right now and it's the PERFECT TIME for you to jump in. If there's one thing I've learnt in the last eight years, it's that when you see a new strategy that's working, you TAKE THE LEAP before thousands of other people start using it.

PART THREE
Case Studies

EMAIL MARKETERS

I LOVE TALKING to people in my industry. Recently I did a bunch of interviews with some of the leading names in email marketing.

I had the same set of questions, but the answers I received blew my mind because they showed me that everyone's story is unique and worth mentioning. The reasons for what they do, and how they do it, gave me a fresh perspective and I hope it helps you, too.

I have had these interviews transcribed and edited. So you'll only read the comments of the marketer I interviewed.

So read these stories, imagining you're having a conversation with the person.

Do not underestimate the lessons revealed in these case studies. If you didn't read the rest of the book and only read these stories that would, in itself, leave a strong impact on the way you think about business.

The following questions were asked to the marketers:

- Please introduce yourself. Tell me a little about

your business and how you got started with Email Marketing.

- How big a role does Email Marketing play in your business?
- Hypothetically—If you had to start all over again. Say you went broke, lost all your contacts and your money. How would you get started?
- What's the first thing a newbie Email Marketer should focus on to setup a profitable Email Marketing campaign?
- What's your opinion on Clickonomy? How does Clickonomy help your business?
- What's the next big thing you're working on?

Some of these marketers got started a couple of years ago and some of them have been in the industry for several years. Some of these marketers have lists of 20,000 or so. Some of them have lists of hundreds of thousands of people.

Read closely and take notes, because you are about to discover different thought processes, different backgrounds, and see different minds converge into one lane: Email Marketing.

KEITH MATTHEW

MY NAME IS Keith Matthew. I am the founder of a few websites—selfmasterysecrets.com, successtribe.com—and I have some other ones, too, but those are my more actively trafficked sites. I've been in personal development since 2007.

I was working a job making $45,000 a year, kind of happy with it because I didn't know otherwise; I didn't have walls or a window, I just was working in a cubicle.

I wanted to make some extra money, so I was selling on eBay and Amazon. I was making about $2,000 a month without a website, just selling books on Amazon. I would go to thrift stores, buy some books, put them up on Amazon and sell them.

I didn't have any merchandise, but I figured out if you find the difference between supply and demand, you can find opportunity. I started seeing opportunity where a Tony Robbins tape set, believe it or not, would go for like $6 sometimes on eBay.

I was disciplined enough not to overspend. I knew what my margins were and how much money I wanted to make. When I say margins, you start out taking a $6 tape set, and you are going to turn it around and put it back up on eBay and sell it for $20.

Those are really good margins. It's not like I was going to become wealthy off of $15 but it was practice. It was practice selling on the Internet.

Then I created an opportunity myself by selling a marketing book. I didn't know who I was going to sell it to, but I sold it to this guy. I recognized his name on the internet and I was like,"He is the author of 'Conversations with Millionaires'," and I'm like, "I'm making $45,000 a year, I'm getting 3 percent pay raises, barely happy, but sure I would like to shake the hand of a millionaire."

I was not going to put that book in the mail.

I was going to save on the shipping, and I was going to walk that book down and shake that man's hand. Eventually I got in the door, and went and shook his hand and gave him his $45 marketing book —the 'Robert Collier Letter Book' is what I sold.

It had been out of print for like 15 years or something. I don't remember the amount of time but it was a long time, and there's this pent-up demand for the book, and he was one of the buyers.

I hand him the book and sit down in his office, and for about 45 minutes we chat about life. I'm telling him what my goals are, and my dreams, and where I see myself.

After 45 minutes he says, "Okay, so that's the end of that, and I'm excited to get started with you." I slid my credit card across his table at his desk and he's like, "Okay, we're going to charge your card with $6,300, and you'll be in our coaching program."

I'm like, "Okay." Then my knees were weak, and it cost me $6,300 to sell a $45 book. But it changed my life, because I put myself in front of someone who is way more successful than me.

Even before the coaching program started, I made myself valuable. I was a graphic designer, and I saw that this guy in Australia was ripping off his CDs, and selling them on eBay as his own. I said, "Look, if this guy is going to rip you off from Australia with these ugly, ugly CD designs, why don't I make some real nice CD designs for you and I'll sell them on eBay for you, and we'll do a partnership?"

And this is a multimillionaire, and it not like it was going to break his bank, but he said yes.

So I started selling his interviews with Jim Rohn, Michael Gerber, Tony Robbins, just all the top names, and this was easy to sell.

You put his name, multimillionaire, along with all these top names and sell them on eBay. They were going like hot cakes, all digital—no physical product.

And it was some lead generation for him, but for me it was a foot in the door of something more.

When you put your money down into a coaching program, there's uncertainty.

It's scary a lot of times, depending on what your budget is. I had some money saved in the bank, so it wasn't going to really make much of a difference to me. Then again, who wants to give away $6,300?

But it's not giving money away, you're investing in your future. You never know when you take a step in a direction and what's going to come from it.

I had no idea when I put the book up on Amazon that I would sell it to a multimillionaire. Then I had no idea when I joined the coaching program what would happen.

A month and a half later I get a call from him and he says, "How do you like your job? Scale of one to ten."

And I'm $45K guy at the time, and I have my vacation time saved, my sick time saved, and I don't really have much in the way of bills.

I'm kind of cool and happy in my little world. I paused, and I said, "I'd say a seven. Yeah, seven."

And he said, "Oh, okay, got you. Well, we were

just talking in the office, and we have an opening here at my company. We thought of you, and we were like, 'Hey, maybe he wants to come work with us?'".

As soon as he said that, I paused and I said, "I'll be there in ten minutes." I was working for a 100-year-old non-profit company where you're supposed to punch in your time clock—punch in, punch out—and I was Mr. Good Worker, $45,000, doing everything you're supposed to do, always have your work done really well, you never have to worry about me.

I said, "I'll be there in ten." I blew past the time clock, got onto the subway train. I was in Manhattan at the time, living tere, working there, and I was down there in no time, and sitting in front of him. I was like, "Here I am".

He goes, "Okay, do you know how to make a website?" I looked at him and I said, "No." He goes, "Do you know how to..." and one after the other he's asking me things that he does in his business or has people do for him. I was like, "No, I don't know how to this, I don't know how to do that." He looks at me and goes, "If I gave you these things to do, could you figure them out?" and I said, "Hell yeah, I could figure them out." He goes, "You're hired!"

For a year I worked for a multimillionaire.

I was one of his right-hand people. For a year, I worked under his wing as an apprentice, as a worker, whatever you want to call it, but I was being trained.

This is night and day. I've seen so many people who try making money online. They want to make a change in their lives, but they don't know how to do it. They take a stab at it and then they don't really get much in the way of results. Then they give up and they go back to their world that they really want to expand and they don't know how to.

For me, I'm working for somebody at the time; this is 2007—I'm working for somebody who knows how to do this stuff.

In fact, the first day I was working there I'm sitting there looking at the screen of his sales, by the way, I got hired as a webmaster. I was supposed to be making webpages and I didn't know what the heck to do.

But when you're willing to make a change in your life, amazing things happen. I put in the hours of having this burden on my shoulders from the stress of trying to figure out how to make webpages, and things were different back then.

It was right after you were learning straight HTML kind of stuff. Now they had some programs, some editors, but today you have things available that in 30 minutes you've got a webpage up. Back then I had no idea what you had to do as a webmaster.

My point is, I'm looking at the screen and I see the sales coming in. It goes $67, $47, $67, $97, $37 and it's streaming like snow or rainfall. It's cascading in, all these sales, constantly.

And so all these people out there who are struggling or were struggling at the time, and they didn't know is this real?; is it a scam?

I didn't have to worry about that because I saw live proof. Holy cow, there's a cascade of money out there. I just have to tap into it.

And after a year doing that, I decided it was time for me to do my own thing. I started my own business and, right out of the gate, I was making more than $100,000 a year because I knew what to do.

When you know how to do this stuff, and it's not rocket science, but if you try to do it on your own, and you don't have somebody guiding you, you can't have a harder time.

I had the wonderful opportunity to learn how to do things correctly.

Whether you are a one-man show, or you have people working under you as a team, your sales drive everything. Whether you're going to pay your rent or your mortgage, or on your car, or pay your bills, or pay your employees, or buy advertising and grow your business.

It's your lifeline, it's your lifeblood. Marketing drives sales. When you have effective marketing in place it makes sales much easier.

And that's a key point; get the marketing down and the sales will follow. You don't even have to worry so much about the sales, marketing is key.

I was surrounded by people who were really good at marketing, and I'm not the best there is. Plenty people are better than me at it, but I know enough good practices to become effective, and I highly recommend that.

When people look to outsource things in their business, I was trained to look at it a different way. I would give up many parts of the business, and the marketing would go last.

I keep a tighter control over giving directions, even if you have a marketer, like a director of marketing or whatever in your company, or someone who is handling it, whatever the title is.

By the way, just on the side real quick. I had so many hats I wore the first year—Director of Marketing, Affiliate Manager, and King of the Universe. It was kind of funny. Every month I had a different hat, so these things—Director of Marketing and blah, blah, blah--they're just a way of categorizing things, it's not such a big deal.

At the end of the day it's about getting things done, and sometimes I wear multiple hats.

But the marketing would be the last thing I would let go of or outsource. Unless, of course, you find somebody who's really good at it.

Like I've seen you're really good at techy stuff, and you have your own product, and you write good copy. You have a really good skill-set. I would hand off, like if you and I were teamed up, I would be happy to hand something off to you before a lot of other people because your marketing is driving your sales.

Clickonomy is very interesting. I remember when it came about, and I was like, "Wow, what is this?" It's a fascinating marketplace that brings buyers and sellers together, people who have a need with people who provide a solution to the need, that is traffic and subscribers and sales, and really just growing your business. Going back to my original training. I'm really good at writing copy, very good at marketing, and so I could drive the traffic. I could drive the leads, and I can help people grow their businesses.

And I do it on a regular basis. I have the

privilege of being able to do it through Clickonomy; some of the results that the people get on Clickonomy are phenomenal.

I tell you, as good as I was when I got my training, these guys on Clickonomy are getting way better results. It's just the way it's set up.

You get some really good sellers, where people who are willing to help others build their businesses and match them up. You're leveraging off the wisdom of all these people in the marketplace of Clickonomy.

For example, I never would want to go under a 40 percent opt-in rate if I was running an advertisement somewhere. Meaning, four out of ten people who click and go visit the webpage give their name and e-mail address or whatever the information is they're asking for.

And that's my own standard. Everybody has their particular standard, but under 40 percent I start wondering. I ask different questions like, "Is it my ad copy?" "Is it the traffic?" "Is it the webpage?"

None of that really comes into play on Clickonomy.

Just yesterday I was talking to a Clickonomy student. He said the first time he ran with me through Clickonomy he got a 70 percent opt-in rate.

That's 70 percent off the bat, that's not

unusual. I have plenty of instances, like more often than not, people are saying to me they are so thrilled to be growing their businesses at such a blistering pace. They are telling what their results are, they're like, "Yeah, I got 60 percent, I got a 70 percent opt-in rate." Some of them are getting 50 percent, but they're getting thousands of people subscribing to their business, and they're getting sales.

The first few times I connected with people through Clickonomy and they bought traffic from me, I didn't know how freaking amazing this was. Then they started telling me, "Yeah, I recouped like two thirds of my money in the first two days." Think about that, you get back most of your money and it's not guaranteed. It's dependent on the advertising campaign and how it's set up.

But more often than not, people are recovering a lot of their invested money. They're gaining thousands of subscribers into their business, and they're pumped.

They're pumped about their future with their businesses, and that's what I'm seeing. They're growing fast, way faster. I put $30,000 into my business when I first started, the first year of having my own company. It was the right thing to do—-I grew my list.

When I was doing it on my own, I didn't have the leverage of Clickonomy back then. These people are growing left and right at such a fast pace. It's one of the reasons why I like being involved in Clickonomy.

My business is really growing well, it has been for years. I'm thrilled with how it is, how my life is. Yet, then I go to Clickonomy and see somebody just starting out, having that same kind of success and life-changing advancement. It makes me feel good.

It makes me feel like I'm giving back, too, while I'm growing myself.

The first steps in getting started? I'd tell people —and I'm going to preface this—the internet changes very quickly. Things change, and you have to keep changing along with what is going on. That said though, right now I recommend people start off with LeadPages. I've been with them for over a year.

A lot of the top people in my industry in personal development, and really excellent marketers, are using LeadPages as well.

It's so quick and easy, and they've done a lot of work for you.

You just click on a bunch of things and you've got a killer webpage up with an opt-in form, and you're good to go on the front end of things.

Case in point, I was in a Mastermind. People pay $5,000 to be at the Mastermind. I was there last week in Connecticut, and a multimillionaire was there; a friend of mine. He was saying the same thing, "Yeah, I use LeadPages all the time."

There's some investment money put up and you can try to do things another way. But I recommend LeadPages because if you try to do things in a bare bones kind of way—and it's pretty reasonable what they are asking in terms of subscription—but if you try to go do it all on your own and you don't tap into the resources that are available to you, you won't be as successful.

Yeah, you may save a couple of a hundred dollars, but it's ultimately going to cost you many thousands of dollars by cutting corners at the beginning. That's what a lot of people don't understand.

And people are in different situations. Some people are strapped for money. Some people have a little cash. What I say to people is, "When you cut a corner in the front of your business when you're just getting started, you save a couple of a hundred of dollars. But if you extrapolate out how much it's going to cost you over the course of a year, or two years, three years--it is staggering."

People don't think this way generally, but I could save a couple hundred dollars and it could cost me $10,000, or more.

Let's say I don't spend $200 or whatever it is. The point is you need something. If you find the solution to solve your problem, then go get it, because that's what it is about.

You want to get from A to B to C, and so if I skimp on $200 then I'm 50 percent less effective over the year.

I'm going to make the numbers up a little bit, because I'm not really a math person per se. But I can make $10,000 in the first year when I could have made $30,000, or $50,000. And with that $50,000, the second year I could have taken $20,000 or $10,000 of that and then put it into advertising.

That advertisement could have turned into 20,000 subscribers, and of those 20,000 subscribers, I might have sold coaching programs for $10,000 or $15,000.

And you just add these numbers up, and it's like, "Oh my god, I'm making $20,000 a year when I could have been making $80,000, or $100,000, or $200,000, but I cut corners at the beginning."

So do it the right way at the beginning and just get it done.

I had the leveraging of a multimillionaire in front of me for a year.

People today have the advantage of many multimillionaires, technology that rocks, the wisdom of people like yourself.

These are people who have made millions of dollars, gone through just about every experience you could go through over the years, and can save you a lot of heartache and just get you right to hitting the bullseye.

So just leverage, leverage, leverage.

I didn't do that for years in certain parts of my business, where I was trying to do things and not leveraging properly. Then suddenly one day, this is like, I already was making a low $100,000 a year, consistently for a few years.

I sat with a multimillion dollar friend of mine back in 2009. We had dinner, and I said, "How do I double my income?"

And he's like, "Email more often."

Because I was only emailing two, three times a week.

He goes, "Email more often and focus on what you're best at. Don't try to do ten things because you can."

Like I used to spend hours on the Warrior

Forum, and you could get lost there just like you could get lost on Facebook for the rest of your life.

I go in there, do what I got to do and get out.

And so I cut out a lot of unnecessary stuff and I focus on the one thing that I'm really, really good at and that's the email marketing—and my income immediately went up.

So talking about lifestyle. It's February. I'm sitting here in front of my pool. Some things about lifestyle people might say are exclusive to email marketing and internet marketing, and I think it might not be. An example is travel. I'm going to Costa Rica for business and fun in a couple of months from now, and that's pretty cool. I've been to New Zealand. I've been all over the place, and it's related to business and I have the freedom to do that, the freedom to do that is real.

The ability to travel is not exclusive to internet marketing. I live in a nice neighbourhood, my neighbours all have million dollar homes here. They could go travel too, and they don't know internet marketing.

If you have an executive position or managerial position, you can be making enough money for paying your bills and living okay.

The difference is how you live your life, though.

The guy next door—he's more likely to not be able to make certain decisions about how he lives his life the way I'm able to make them as someone who does email marketing and internet marketing.

Case in point, we were messing around with the Google Chat and Google Hangouts, which we're doing here. I'd never done it before and you were very patient. I'm sitting out at my pool, and I'm messing around with Hangouts and having fun.

It's new to me so I have a learning curve with it, technology and everything, but we figured it out. I had the opportunity to learn something new, whereas I didn't have to go and say, "Hey boss, can I go learn something new for a few minutes?"

I don't have to ask for permission in my life.

It is 11:30--it's been raining here--but it is 11:30 in the morning, and I can do whatever I want to do.

And then I said, "Hey, you know what, I want bring one of my dogs over to daycare."

I like to have them with me. I have them at the pool and everything, but one of the puppies, he got neutered on Friday. So he's got this cone, and he's running around, he's knocking things over with the cone.

They like to play, and I've got to keep him

away from the other one because they can't play fight. He can't get wet, he can't be by the pool, and he can't get riled up. So I sent the other one off to daycare so he can go play with his dog friends over across town.

I don't care about the money because I got plenty of it.

A lot of people listening to this are going to be like, "I want to have that kind of situation, where I don't care about the money."

I value money I honour money; but what I'm saying is that it comes in so quickly, I can't spend it fast enough.

I can just basically do whatever I want to do.

If I want my dog to be happy, to have a certain experience, I go send him off and don't worry about it.

My puppies are very important to me, they are my joy. I take them to the dog park in the middle of the day. People are working at their jobs and I'm off at the dog park playing with my dogs.

Which brings out a bigger issue. People who have children or have loved ones, have a girlfriend, have a wife, have a husband. This is like the biggest travesty in me, because we are human beings, and we're working all the time if we have jobs.

I know it because I was there.

You commute back and forth every day, commuting alone for a lot of people is a grind and a wear.

And I didn't even know how much it was a grind on me until I stopped, when I finally quit and started my own business.

I was like, "Oh my God, I have so much more energy because I don't have to contend with all this stuff just to get to go."

I don't have to do any of that, and the travesty is we're human beings on this planet made to love each other. Yes, we have to make our way, but we're here to love each other. We're here to give something to the world. And how can you do that? How can you love your wife, or your husband, as much as you possibly want, when you're hardly seeing them?

Because you're both working all the time and, if you have kids, you get home from a long day of work, you're probably tired, you've got the kids to take care of, they have to do their homework.

But you have this life that's just compressed. You have 24 hours, and your valuable part of your life is compressed into like an hour or something.

Now, I'm not saying you can't have joy at work, too. There are people who love what they're doing at work, but I have the ability to love who I want to love, how I want to love them.

I could be with my dogs 24/7, or I can go let them play with their pack. They have their own social life.

Having your own business in internet marketing and email marketing, where the money flows so quickly, that's given me the ability to do that.

I want to thank you for what you're doing, and reaching out to all the people you're reaching out to and the lives you're about to change.

Someone changed my life one time, and for the remainder of my days I live differently now because someone was able to do that for me.

And I want to thank you for what you're doing for everybody with Clickonomy. I guarantee you anyone who comes to Clickonomy and wants to work with you, and wants to grow their businesses, they can find me - Keith Matthew - and I will help them personally.

I'll help you get your ad copy put together and your campaign.

I'll look it over and make sure that's going to rock it out.

And I wish for everybody the best, and also that you get to be with the loved ones that you want to be with, and live the life that you want to live.

When you have that, you're freed up to live your life purpose because you don't have to worry about the money. Then you can start giving to society the way you want to give, and make an imprint to our society and change people's lives yourself. I wish that for everybody.

ANIK SINGAL

I STARTED IN the business about 13 years ago. I fell into it by complete mistake. I was sitting in college—miserable. I didn't want to go to classes and all that.

I didn't want to go get a job. It sounded crazy to me to slave and go to class every day and spend all this money.

I was spending $20,000 a year on education. Now, I did graduate. I did get my degree. My dad damn well made sure of that.

But it didn't make sense. All that for what? To get a job that would be $35,000, $40,000 a year to start, and again, be slaving?

I just felt like I'd always be a slave. I'll just be a slave to other people. Here I report to teachers and professors in my college, later I'd be reporting to my boss and to the company.

It's not what I wanted. I always found myself to be very entrepreneurial.

I wanted to do something that allowed me to impact the world and allowed me to have my own—

take ownership of my life, dictate my own schedule, wake up when I want to wake up, travel the world, do what I want to do.

So, you know, I was very entrepreneurial since I was a kid and I decided that's the route I should go. Now, here's the problem with it, though. I had about $100 to my bank account and last time I checked, you can't go out and buy a franchise with $100.

So, I was a little lost. I didn't even know about this whole concept of making money on the internet. I was one of those guys who went to Google and typed in the words "make money" and I saw all the usual scams. I saw the stuffing envelopes, survey answers, all this nonsense—luckily didn't buy any of it.

I found my way to this forum that talked about internet marketing. It talked about making money on the internet and I thought, "Ooh, I have internet. I have a computer. I'm at university at one of the best internet connections. I can do this".

Here I was—it was just this vortex—it was this whole other dimension. I just fell into it and I got addicted. I got sucked in completely. I never turned back after that and it changed my life.

I would spend more time on the forums than I did anything else. I became completely anti-social.

Five, six, seven hours a day, I would spend just learning; but that's what you had to do back then. There was no mentor back then to teach us this stuff and to train us.

I literally sat, I tested, tried, tried, tried, learned, saw what everyone's doing. I could see 100 people take pieces of their puzzles and put them together. Every time I thought I had it, and I thought I figured it out, I failed.

In 18 months, I didn't make a penny—failed, failed, failed, failed, over and over again. Finally, that one morning, I woke up and discovered a system that worked for me.

Later on, months after that, I discovered the world of email. I tripled the money I was making.

Since then, I've never looked back. I've had bad days. I've had times when I almost went bankrupt and my company fell apart.

Not because of the business, but because I made bad decisions as a CEO. And always, the one thing that saved me, the one thing that saved my business, was email.

If I didn't have an email list, I wouldn't be sitting in front of you today. I would have gone out of business, and been broke, many, many, many times over the last 13 years.

I never would have broken seven figures. This year we're going to do probably 20 to 25 million dollars. Maybe 30.

I'm trying to be conservative here, not to get my own hopes up. And I'll tell you that 90 percent of that income, if not more, is because of email. So, email is very important and it has no ceilings.

We're already doing eight figures. I know for a fact, I can do nine. And I can do ten. I can do billions of dollars on the internet using email. I'm so proud of you for deciding to make email a big part of your business because it's completely transformational.

I've taught more than 150,000 students and we've figured out what works the best and what works the quickest.

I fell, at one point, seven million dollars into debt. I was down and out.

I had to bring myself back out. So what did I do? How did I save my company, save my life, save my future, financially? Email list.

So what I would do today, if I had to start all over again, is I would go as simple as putting up an opt-in page. A one-page website, which now is so easy to create. It's just a template system.

A onepage website. Tie it together with an auto-responder. Again, these technologies are available left, right, and center.

Click, click, no technology experience. It's super easy. Back then it wasn't. Now it's become so automated.

And I would simply pick offers off a service like ClickBank. I wouldn't sit and make my own products, I would just sit and pick other people's offers.

And I would take $500. I don't care what I have to do to get that $500. I would work at McDonald's if I have to. I would go ask my grandmother if I had to. I would try not to borrow money, but I would go out and do a job.

Go out and find something. Help a friend move. Put something up on Craigslist. I hate it when I hear people say, "I don't have $300 to invest in traffic."

Yeah you do—you just haven't tried!

I would do whatever I had to do to get $500 to invest in traffic.

I would go to Clickonomy.com. I would put that $500 in there, I'd buy a solo ad.

I would buy a good solo ad, drive it, get leads to opt into my Opt-In Page, and promote affiliate offers to it.

I would be religious about mailing my list every

day. I probably would avoid mailing on a Friday and a Saturday. So if you decide you're going to mail your list five days a week, it's the only two days you skip, Friday and Saturday. If you want to mail your list six days a week, skip Friday.

If you want to mail your list seven days a week, that's fine, too. It's a discipline. It's a religion. You cannot stop. You have to do it every day.

When your list is tiny and small, there will be days when you make no money. There might be days where you only drive 80 clicks, and you don't get a sale.

It doesn't matter.

The next day you mail again.

The day after that you mail again, because soon enough your list is going to be much bigger, and every day you'll make sales.

And on days that you don't mail, you won't make sales.

So that's it. That's the system, and I believe that that's exactly what you're teaching as well.

First, I want to start by telling everybody that Ritoban is modest. Without him, Clickonomy wouldn't exist.

I believe it's one of my most brilliant creations.

I think Ritoban and I have created something

that is going to revolutionize the entire industry. I am not exaggerating.

This company is going to change lives. This service is finally going to make it possible for people who initially were scared or found it difficult to make money online.

Facebook, Google, Bing and Yahoo are all excellent places, all places I'm getting traffic from now, too. But they're not good places to start. They're confusing. They need time to learn.

What you really want to do is something simple with instant results that you know you can count on.

I always tell my students, "Go get solo ads. Do email media. Buy sponsorship ads. Look, there's already so many people who have email lists. Just buy an ad in there.

So the next question I get is, "How do I find these people?" And I'll say, "Come on, you just go to Google, type it in. Get on Skype, talk to people, ask for referrals."

Easy for me, easy for us. But people who are just beginning are like, "What ?" They're scared or timid or shy to talk to people.

How do I know if that person's good? What if he scams me? What if he doesn't convert? And how do I know I can trust him and how do I even find him? How do I talk to him? What if he takes advantage of me?

I was hearing it over and over and, anytime there is a problem for an entrepreneur, that's an opportunity. And so I really sat down and I thought, "It's not easy, it won't be easy at all. In fact, it'll be really hard."

But let me figure out what I can do to just make it so that this problem never happens. No one ever says anything about this. That's where the Clickonomy idea came from. Then you took over and just lit it on fire and built all this extra stuff.

Nobody can join Clickonomy and say they don't have a list. You've no excuse to because you're just one solo ad buy away from having a list.

It's instant, it's guaranteed. You will get an email list. Everyone else who's bought from that seller leaves comments and reviews. So you can feel trust.

The money you invest with the seller goes to us first. It's a common escrow so you feel good.

This was a service we really did for people who are just beginning to give you the assurance you need to make you sleep at night; knowing you're getting great traffic and you're protected by Ritoban and myself.

No one can hurt you, you're part of our team now and you're part of this VIP group. I'm so proud of what we've done while we're still in Alpha mode.

We've done more than a half a million clicks while we're just playing around, building it, learning it. Now it's officially graduated to the Beta level.

We're about to really turn the fire on. There are more than 130 sources for you to buy in traffic.

Weight loss, fitness, personal development, internet marketing, business opportunities, the list goes on. Every day we're adding more and more people. Clickonomy is about to go official. That means the bigger it is, the more sellers you can choose from, the cheaper the rates you get.

It's an open marketplace. It's a free market. So the more people who get involved, the more you benefit from it because the prices fall, and we don't charge anything to the buyer. I believe it's one of those rare opportunities where we get a win-win-win.

We've created a three-way win opportunity here. My vision for us is we're going to deliver 100 million clicks and we are going to change at least ten thousand lives.

Ten thousand people are going to be starting their digital marketing, email marketing business because of the fact that Clickonomy existed. That is gonna be what changes the industry completely and that's my big vision for it.

Three tips for those who are just starting out.

Tip number one: Do not waste the thank you page. If you waste the thank you page, you're losing a lot of money.

Someone just came to your website. They saw something. They read it. They put their e-mail address in—you know they actually took time on the internet.

This is a big deal, because you can just click, click, click everything.

They took time to click on something, type their e-mail address, share something personal with you, and hit submit. They just voted. They said, "I like you."

What happens on the next page is you go and say, "Thank you. Check your email. See you later."

Imagine someone walked up to you on the street and said, "Hey, how are you?" and shook your hand and you said, "Yeah, thanks. See you."

How rude is that?

They just showed you they're interested. You owe it to them to interact with them more. Put up a video. Even if it's not you, put up an affiliate product. Monetize that.

You're going to make the most money right at

the spot. It will help you recover your investment, so it will help you scale your traffic. You can buy more traffic.

Tip number two: I can't say this more strongly. I know you're going to forget this advice, so many of you do this, but please try not to.

Mail daily.

I know when your list is small in the beginning, it sucks because you mail and you see no results, you see no money. Sometimes two, three, four days go by.

Let's not forget, if your email list is only a thousand, fifteen hundred, or two thousand big, you're probably only generating 30, 40, 50 clicks per email. Maybe 100 clicks.

When that list gets to be 50, 60, 70, 80 thousand—every day when you email—you're guaranteed to print money.

Get in the habit now. Make it a religious practice to mail your list every single day.

Number three: Keep things different. Keep things unique. I never send out the same messages. Some of my messages are short. Some of my messages are big and long. Some are stories. Some are direct sales. Some are a link to a video. Some are a link to my blog. Some are a link to a survey.

I want to activate them. Sometimes people start

to fall away when you do too much of the same stuff. They ignore it. Suddenly one day, you say, "Subject line: giving away a free iPad." All of a sudden, people are like, "Oh, what is he doing? I'll get involved in that."

Get creative with how you approach your lists: thank-you page, mail daily, and change up the kinds of emails you send to your list. Don't do the same thing every day because if you do, your results will drop.

Email lifestyle? I'll put it in one word: freedom. We talk about financial freedom. Everybody says, "I want financial freedom. I want financial freedom."

And so they think being an entrepreneur means financial freedom.

When I first became an entrepreneur, I worked twice as hard, if not harder, than if I just had a job. You know when you're an entrepreneur, people will start a physical business, like a store.

How is that freedom? I don't understand. You have to check in every day for 10 to 12 hours. You have to hire employees, you have to deal with their hustles.

You become a consultant. Now you have a client hounding on you every single day to get work done.

How is that freedom? These things aren't freedom and what impact are you making? If you're a contractor or consultant, you are what? You're talking to one person helping one person. Right?

When you're an email marketer, you have people who have joined your list from all over the world and you're reaching them and impacting their lives.

You could be sitting on a beach. You could be sitting in front of a computer at your home. You could be sitting on a vacation.

Things have happened in my life that were very bad. I ended up in the hospital. I was on my death bed a couple of times.

I ran my business from the ICU using my phone. That's all I used. I typed out an email out and I still was having a voice to the world. I still was generating revenue.

You change the world, have a voice to the world, impact people's lives while truly attaining freedom for yourself because there is no boss, there is no one telling you what to do, you don't have to check in.

If you want to go on a 10-day vacation, you don't even need to type a single email.

Type 10 emails, pre-log them and go on

vacation. You never even have to log in and check. The auto-responder will send those emails for you.

Ritoban is one of my closest friends. He's like a little brother to me. He is also a business partner, but I'll tell you, he's one of our best best best best best best students. You could not be in better hands.

This guy is brilliant. Just the other day I remember telling him he is, by far, the most talented person I've ever met in my life. That includes myself, and so you couldn't be in better hands.When he says something, listen to him, and execute.

And do what he says.

All the best on your efforts with email marketing. I wish you all the best. And I know you'll kill it. Just keep working hard. And remember, email every day. It's very important. Talk to you soon.

BILL WHITE

I STARTED IN advertising 20 years ago and it was as a graphic artist in rather large marketing agencies.

It was a somewhat interesting career, but required me to work 60 to 100 hours a week. I just felt that wasn't sustainable over the long term and certainly not in alignment with my goals.

Eleven years ago, I started my corporation and I ran it entirely in the background of my career for quite some time.

Initially, I was in the personal development space. I developed a few products and launched them into ClickBank. This is obviously quite a long time ago, when the internet was a very different climate.

I kind of ran it as a part-time business for many years and then, when the economic downturn happened, I found myself being progressively downsized. I had to jump around from job to job for a while.

It was just a matter of diminishing returns. So I looked to the business I had been building in the background for a long time and said, "I'm going to have to scale this up."

So, for about four years now, I have been into full time internet marketing. It's spread out into the health niche, which is also another passion of mine. That pretty much sums it up.

Ever since, I love email marketing and a lot of content marketing, various formats and methods across the webpages in the social media channels.

The best way to build an email list, and it's changed over time versus when I first got into internet marketing—this was prior to CAN-SPAM legislation —the rules were a lot different.

Single opt-in was really the norm and double opt-in didn't come in until after I'd been marketing for a while. In this day and age, I would say a lot of people do double opt-in.

I would go single opt-in, it's still a viable option. It's not typically publicized through most of the email services like AWeber, but the option is there. That certainly speeds up list-building.

If I was starting at ground zero again, if I had no list and I was building a list, it just basically grows as fast as you are willing to purchase solo ads or other forms of advertising to build your list.

You have to have a good opt-in page with a

compelling offer. You have to have your
autoresponder system set up. You have to get familiar
with how to use that, whether it's sending
autoresponder sequences or broadcast emails.

But getting people into the funnel is really the
name of the game. That's the bottom line of what's
going to dictate whether you're profitable or not, and
it's a process.

There are free methods out there to do it. You
can get into giveaways and do swaps with people. But
you have to have an initial list to really access that
because you have to be able to send traffic as well as
receive it.

So, I really believe paid solos are probably the
quickest method and, obviously, it's dictated by your
budget. But typically you'll do well if you set up your
opt-in page efficiently, you get good conversion rates
on that and you have a good back-end offer on your
landing page, which would be the page after someone
enters their name and email address, and clicks, "Yes,
I want your gift," or whatever.

Give a good, compelling offer on the back end
of that, you usually can recoup your money pretty
reliably and pretty quickly. That's really the fastest
way to scale up, you send out a solo, you make the
money back with your back-end offer and then you

just rinse-repeat.

You just keep doing it until your list gets incrementally larger. Then you'll, of course, follow up with the other offers through your autoresponder sequence or doing broadcast emails to your list.

Where I think people really miss it is the opt-in page. If you don't have strong copy on there, strong headline, a compelling offer, you want it to look cosmetically easy on the eye, but you basically have to kind of get into the mind of your customer and say, "What can I put in front of my potential customer that I'm going to give them for free that they're just not going to be able to say no to?"

I have quite a few funnels myself. Opt-in pages that go anywhere from 35-40 percent conversion rate all the way up to, I think the highest one ever had was 89 percent, which is pretty remarkable.

The main emphasis is getting that opt-in page to a point that you basically want an offer someone can't refuse and then put that into solos or other means.

With solo ads, you're going to list owners who already have a list. They're recommending or inadvertently endorsing you when they mail to their list, so those people are very likely to click the links in the email and go over to see what it is that you have in the offer.

It's very, very efficient, but, like I said, the critical component in that, too, is you have to have a good back-end to offer on that landing page. You want to make some of your advertising cost back—you buy a solo, you make the money back, you buy another solo and then each time you do that, you're growing your list.

And once you have that list, you can market to them, again and again, so that each time one of your people on the list buys, that increases the value of your list. You are making more and more money off the same people by providing them more and more products.

Clickonomy has been a very, very great revenue source for me in terms of giving me yet another outlet. I used to sell primarily ClickBank products and other affiliate products. But being able to monetize my list in another way has been very productive for me. It's also given me the opportunity to give back in a way to the up-and-coming members of the internet marketing community.

One of the main things I love to do when I have a client on Clickonomy is take a look at that opt-in page and say, "You know, maybe you can change your headline to this," or "Maybe if you change this font over here." Every time you get a kind of feel for what kind of copy is going to convert well or what kind of page layout is going to convert well.

So, I like to spend that initial contact with my customers through Clickonomy and say, "Let's take a look at your opt-in page. Let's look at your giveaway." Sometimes I download the PDF gift, or whatever kind of gift they have. I explore that a little bit and make recommendations so they have a greater success rate from the beginning. I think that that's really important.

I'm not talking about getting millions of dollars every night, but when you start to see steady incremental growth in your business from the very onset, it keeps you motivated.

It keeps you very enthusiastic about growing your business. It really gets you to the stage where you can really see where this could, at some point, replace or even surpass your career.

And Clickonomy has just been a remarkable vehicle for that—both in terms of adding another revenue stream for my own business as well as allowing me, through that medium, to help others grow their business. Then they can enjoy their financial freedom and the time freedom, which is really what I love about this the most, that I own my time.

I live just north of Dallas, Texas. It's a very large metropolitan area. As a former graphic artist who worked in advertising, my normal schedule would have been to get up relatively early in the morning and do the whole morning ritual of shower, shave and breakfast.

And then get into traffic and sit in gridlock for an hour and twenty minutes on the way to an office. There I would sit anywhere from the rare eight-hour day to typically a ten, twelve, fourteen-hour day. Then I get to go back into gridlock , come home and then try to squeeze out a little bit of living in between the evenings and weekends.

I'm a family man. I have a son, he's in middle school now about to go to high school next year. So it limited the amount of time I could be involved in my son's life and limited the amount of time I could pursue my personal passions.

By contrast, now I don't have to do that anymore. I get up pretty much whenever I want to. I tend to stay up late, so a lot of times I queue up emails and do my business sometimes at two or three in the morning.

I would say my average workday is somewhere around half an hour to an hour. Then I may check email periodically through the day or I might have some particular project I am working on.

It's really more of a project-oriented lifestyle.

At some point, you may develop your own products or you may be spending time adding content for your blog or content for social media channels or things like that.

But I'm a really pro-active guy. So, for example, I might write six months' worth of articles over a period of two weeks and post them all up to my blog. Then I will let them drip out with the WordPress feature that allows you to schedule blog posts.

I'm an avid painter and I'm a musician. I've got a 32-track recording studio right here at home. So I spend time playing guitar or writing music or painting or cooking.

I have a garden at the back, so I garden a lot. It's almost like been semi-retired, honestly.

I'm an organic gardener here at the house and so health has been very important to me. I work out four days a week and I think if you don't have your health, everything else kind of suffers.

It's something I am passionate about—clean and healthy living and just being able to feel good enough; having the energy and staving off the aging process long enough to actually pack some enjoyment into life.

I've just really been wanting to focus more on penetrating all of the media channels possible.

We have Twitter, Facebook, Pinterest, Instagram, YouTube. Penetrating on the social media platforms with some content that people actually want to share a lot and discuss a lot and get excited about has really been my primary focus in terms of increasing the amount of traffic to my own funnels and giving me alternative streams to keep more and more customers going in. Business is definitely growing.

I think the economy is starting to turn a bit. I don't know if it's that people just got tired of the economic downturn and said, "Hey, I'm going to spend money again because I got to live," or if we're actually recovering, but I've definitely seen upward trends.

It's really not about the money. You can work 60 or 100 hours a week in this business if you want to.

There's an old proverb that says 'a rich man knows when he has enough'.

I don't need a Rolex on my wrist. I'm not interested in driving a Jag. It's not that I'm opposed to those things, but I put a lot of value on having that "free time." I spend more quality time with my son than any working man in the corporate world could even conceivably give to their child.

So, I think that's another thing, too, just the quality time that you get to spend with the people you love is pretty incredible.

You can follow the paradigms we're all raised up to believe in; work hard and get a job and you will be okay kind of thing. Or you can break into a new paradigm and just say, "I'm going to take control of my life and live it on my terms." We only get to live this life one time.

No matter what your theological beliefs are, even if you're going to live again, you're not going to live as this person that you're today.

Seize the moment and take control of your life and this is definitely a way that you can do it—that I can personally attest works. You'll get out of it what you put into it.

Anything I've ever done, this has been the most consistently reliable way to create the life I wanted. I think it's possible for anyone who really wants it.

JIMMY KIM

MY NAME IS Jimmy Kim. I'm based in San Diego, California and I've been doing internet marketing since 2009. I've got multiple companies built out.

I've got my affiliate marketing company, but my big baby right now is my email marketing company, SendLane. SendLane is an email service provider, kind of like GetResponse, AWeber, ConstantContact, iContact—just to put out a couple of names to you, just to create familiarity.

I've done a lot of things online from product launches to email marketing to Facebook and other paid advertisement methods.

I was fortunate enough to have a teacher and a mentor, a well-known one actually, that most of you guys would know - Anik Singal.

I had him as one of my mentors who helped me learn how to do internet marketing at one point or another. My first dollar came online probably from SEO.

I used to learn and understand how SEO

works. Because I was connected with everybody in the industry, through Anik, I was able to learn what products names were before the products came out.

I would do like really aggressive SEO, not knowing what I was doing. I remember the first day I made that first $100. It was really cool to do it and I realized it could work.

So from there, I've evolved. I've been able to grow my business every year.

I was looking at our gross chart with my CPA just recently and I saw that every year I've brought more than 100 percent. This last year I did more than $3 million net, so I was really excited.

It was a really exciting point in my life and I've continued to grow.

So now I know I have a big challenge this year in 2015. I know I'm way behind the eight ball already because I've been trying to shift gears again this year because I'm growing this bigger company.

I own a clothing brand store now. Also with my internet marketing stuff, I'm shifting niches right now. Right now I do personal development. I've done internet marketing stuff and I've done some biz-opp stuff, and I want to continue to expand my marketing.

When you expand, unfortunately, you slow down a little bit before you can speed up. So, I'm in my slow down period this year right now. But I did it intentionally in the beginning of the year because I now want to end the year with a big bang.

Internet marketing's a huge role of mine. I actually have a really fun case study, back in, I think it was August of this past year, 2014. I actually wanted to get into the personal development market. I had my know-how, what I've done and how I've done what I've done, but I didn't have a list. I didn't have a name.

I kind of did a case study. It was actually for my own good. The idea behind the case study was really just for me because I wanted to see that I could do it in any niche. Because if I know I can do it in this niche, then I can do it in any niche.

Back in August I started with a zero list, no squeeze pages, nothing. I had nothing.

But really the idea and process behind building a list is really much easier than people think it is. So fast forward. I'm going to go back into what I did, but fast forward to this day from back then. I've got a list of more than 65,000 now in the personal development space I've built.

Now, I've earned my money all back, I've made money with that, and I've been able to continue to grow that list.

So what did I do back then? I did multiple things.

I started off by purchasing solo ads, real simple. I was using your platform Clickonomy, and I was able to start purchasing solo ads.

I mean there was really good traffic in there, really good sources of traffic, and really good people in there.

So, I was able to buy traffic. By then I started building my list and I started to grow.

I think I grew to about 7,000 using Clickonomy. Then I was able to use my experience with Facebook and I was able to purchase ads through Facebook.

I was basically in everyone's face on Facebook for months at a time. I was spending about $100 a day to get about 114 to 118 subscribers a day.

I was targeting things like Law of Attraction, The Secret, big names like Bob Proctor and Anik Singal. Basically going out there, attacking, and being in front of everybody who likes personal development stuff.

Then the third thing I did was I got involved heavily in swaps. A lot of different swap opportunities were out there. Or just swaps where I go to other people who have lists and say, "Hey, I want to send you x amount of clicks and you send me x amount of clicks and we have a swap."

So from there it grew exponentially to the point where my list is now responsive enough, and big enough, that I can get on leaderboards on big offers.

I'm making some money. Just a week ago or so ago the last promotion I did was with Sonia Ricotti. I placed second on her weekend contest, and I made about five, six grand in commission with that offer.

That's really good, considering that six months ago I didn't even have this list.

I'm making about $15,000 to $18,000 a month with my personal development list that I built six months ago. That's the proof in the pudding that I know what I'm doing. I've done it, and what I've done was nothing out of the ordinary, nothing hard.

It was just about putting in a little bit of time, taking the action and doing it. That's all it was.

Doing the work to get there. These steps are taught by everybody. It's not like I had secret knowledge in what I did. What I did was exactly what people tell you to do.

Go to the squeeze page, give them something for free, and put them in an auto-responder and mail it.

Buy solo ads, buy Facebook ads, do swaps. It's

really simple and straight-forward. I look at it and I go, "Wow, what I've learned in the last five, six, years, I've been able to apply in the last six months. I've been able to add another $15,000 to $20,000 a month income stream to my life, just like that."

This year I wanted to continue to add more income streams. Why not?

Keep adding income streams of $15,000 to $20,000. Some people make that amount in an entire year. I'm able to do that with very minimal work.

I'm not putting any effort and time into it, maybe 30 minutes a day into that business.

Take 30 minutes times, let's say, five days a week, times 25 days, 30 minutes a week. I'm putting in like 12-and-a-half hours a month.

That's how easy it can be if you can systematize the process. Now, I'm not saying it would be easy for everybody to do what I've been able to do. This isn't something that's doable overnight, but it's experience and time that get you there.

I was having a conversation with a friend the other day about this, what we do and what we've been able to do as email marketers. There's two ways we felt you could look at it. You could look at it as a lifestyle business, or you could look at it as being able to have a sustainable income at all times of your life. All the while you would be able to grow to the next level with everything.

When I first started doing this, my idea behind everything was building a lifestyle business. Basically, travel, buy toys, live the big life, and not have to do a lot of work.

I did that for a while. It was really fun. I basically could hangout and just email my list, go buy a watch. If I wanted to buy this watch I would say, "Okay. If email three times, four times, five times this week, I can buy that watch at the end of the week." That's how I felt.

So I used to use that idea, and that's how I lived my life. That's where I was a couple of years ago but, unfortunately, because I'm an entrepreneur, I get bored. I got bored with the lifestyle life.

I got bored with that idea of doing nothing and just simply making money, and just living life. To some people, that's excellent and if that's what you want to do, more power to you. I love it, because I know friends who make seven figures online doing that and just living life travelling.

For me, I've been in a different boat now.

I've been wanting to grow something bigger, better, stronger, and that's where SendLane comes in.

That's been basically taking one of my passions

in life, which has been marketing, and taking it and helping others in that world. Not only helping, but being able to build a large, big vision company with it.

Our idea behind it is basically helping deliver email, but putting everything under a roof of marketers who understand marketing.

A lot of these email marketing companies out there, unfortunately, don't understand the marketing concept: affiliate marketers, digital marketers—the kinds that you and I are. They don't understand that so we wanted to build a company that's wrapped around that. That's been my big vision now.

Basically, my lifestyle with email marketing is: I wake up in the morning, I email, and then I work on my big business.

It's given me the flexibility to do what I want. I look back at my history, and one of the things I always talk about and preach about is the fact that, before I got into internet marketing in 2009, I actually had a really different type of life.

I was in the car sales industry. I didn't start there. I started off back in the early 2000s washing cars, and from there moved up through the ranks.

I moved up the ranks from washing cars, to selling cars, to being the salesman of the month, to being a sales manager, to finance manager, until eventually having my own store, which is amazing.

I was one of the youngest general managers in the nation at the age of 25. But when you work 80 hours a week and you don't see much return, I mean, I look back and I'm like, "Okay, so I was working like 60 to 80 hours a week minimum. I was running a store. I was running three stores at one point. I looked at how much money I was making compared to what I do now. It's amazing how different it is."

I used to stress myself. I'd have hair falling out. I'd have to wear a suit every day. Today, I'm sitting here in this Batman shirt. I don't care what I wear because it doesn't matter. I can do this internet thing from home.

What you're seeing behind me is my home office. I don't have to commute. I still make way more money than I used to make.

So when I left that business, I actually took a big leap of faith. I actually took a pay cut to come and learn internet marketing. Why did I do that?

Because I realized I want to do something bigger in my life than just sit behind the desk and work for someone else. So that's when I met Anik, my mentor. He was kind of living that lifestyle life as well, one that I wanted.

You see it. I'm sure you've seen it. We all see it.

There's a lot of these internet marketers who are out there, who are email marketers, they just flaunt their life.

They go out and they're like, "Oh, I'm going to Italy next week, then I'm in Australia next week. I'm driving my Ferrari." You know what I mean?

It sounds incredible, but it's true. It really is true. These people are out there doing this because they can do this, and they have a lifestyle business in that way. So it really depends.

My outlook on it is, if you want just a lifestyle, you can have it with email marketing.

It really isn't a lot of work once you systematize it, like I have with my last thing about my personal development list.

If I'm a normal Joe Schmoe and I've been able to make from two to four grand a month to 15 to 20 grand, I can live my lifestyle business. I told you how much work I've put into it.

It was 12-and-a-half hours a month into my business, and the rest of the time I'm just playing. Imagine that.

Now let's put 25 hours in this, so let's double the time I put in. Why couldn't I make 30 to 40 grand in that month?

It just goes off from there. It's a really easy

snowball effect. There are growth levels and things you've got to hit, but it's not hard at all.

These things are easy, it's just about systems. As you said, it's step-by-step.

When I first started back in 2009, I don't believe I was given these steps and systems that are available these days. If I had what is available nowadays, all the automation, all the email marketing tools, all this stuff, I would be able to have done it so much faster.

I look back, and that's what I laugh about. Because back then, to build a landing page you had to go online, go find someone who would design it for you, put all the words in, test everything, put the forms in.

It was like a nine, ten step process.

These days, for example with SendLane, we created a landing page builder. You just go and click on things. You just click on the different pages and you type in what you want, and then you say link it to my squeeze page. Guess what? Your squeeze pages are online within two minutes.

It's tied to your responders, it's tied to your list already. You don't have to do anything, and it's self-posted. These are the things you can get these days. You don't have to worry about hosting, domain names. You don't have to worry about any of that anymore.

It's really the systems and steps out there that make life easier. Doing internet marketing now, in 2015, is easier than ever. It's something you can put into work. It's something I feel that anybody can do who really is serious about taking some action and doing something different in their life, though it be a lifestyle, or building a big business, or whatever they want to do, or it could even just be taking care of the family.

It doesn't matter. Spend more time with your family and make more money online, and have more time for yourself and your life, too. It could be whatever you want to do.

With SendLane, our main goal was to simplify, from our UI to the features we have built in, and to pricing.

We wanted to make it a feature in which you felt that when you purchased SendLane, you weren't just getting just a bare email marketing system.

We wanted you to have everything you needed to get started. We have a landing page builder. It's built into the system where we're actively adding templates to it. I think we've got about seven or eight now. You can build your own templates. You don't

have to integrate, go third party and worry about it.
We're all doing it for you.

Number two—we'll host it for you, or you
could download it.

Basically, if you want to put it on your domain,
you're welcome to. We give you the raw HTML files,
you just download and upload and then hit install and
it's on.

Or you can just use their self-hosted links. We
have links, it's loaded right on our site and it's live
instantly. That's really cool.

Then we also have our automations. As email
marketers, I want the ability to control my
subscribers.

Automation for us is a little bit different. If
people subscribe to your list, you have options. If they
get the email and they click on it, then you put them
into this sequence. If they don't click on it, you put
them into this sequence.

If they click on this, you put them into a
different list. If you don't click on this, you do it here.
If they don't click here, you can send them there.

It's kind of like a big, giant spider web you can
develop.

Let's say you send an email and they don't
respond to that first email, so let's put them to that

second email. Let's get a little more aggressive about it. Let's put them to a third email and get even more aggressive until, let's say, 10 emails from now, they're just not opening your emails. They don't care.

Then we realize, "Hey, they don't need to be on my list. Let's unsubscribe them from the list." That sounds scary that you have to delete. But guess what? If they didn't open in 10 emails, they are not going open in 20, they are not going to open in 40. They're just wasting space in here.

Just remember your email list is like your real estate. It's basically your online digital real estate. That's what you own, and sometimes you have to let little pieces of that real estate go because they are unnecessary. It's like bad bits, it's like a hill or it's like a dirt, or something that you don't need any more.

We have active smart monitoring and smart hygiene. A lot of people don't know that in email marketing after 90 days if parts of your list aren't responsive, you should get rid of them. It's not uncommon for me to go off and delete a hundred-thousand emails.

That sounds scary to anybody, deleting a hundred-thousand emails off your email list. I just did it about a week ago. You have to do it because those hundred-thousand people haven't opened your email in the last 90 days.

What makes you think in the next 90 days they are going to open your email? They're not. They've gone. They no longer care.

So you get rid of them and it helps your deliverability because your list gets smaller, your message doesn't get sent to as many places, and your reputation increases because you have more people click on your links.

If you have 100 thousand people, and you're getting a 10 percent open rate, you have 10 thousand people to open your list. Now, just imagine if you were able to cut 50 thousand people off that list. Now you have 50 thousand people, but you still have 10 percent opening that same email. Now, you have an overall 20 percent open rate.

So, what happens? Your reputation increases. Then, they say, "Oh, maybe your email was going to someone's spam box for one reason or another." Then they'll start dropping into their inboxes because they're like, "Oh, well, this person's delivering really good content. So let's try to put him into inboxes and see what happens."

And suddenly you'll see your increase go from 10 percent or 20 percent, to 25 percent or 30 percent.

There's a lot of thingswe offer inside of

SendLane to make these things happen really easily with a click of a button. Because we're digital marketers. Because we're internet marketers.

We know how to make the best out of it. We try to provide all the tools. We're working on some tutorials and everything we can do to grow it.

We take suggestions from our customers. We constantly are upgrading the UI. Upgrading this, upgrading that. Just trying to figure out the best way to make SendLane the best email marketing company out there.

It's a slow growth.

Our number one focus right now is customer service.

I learned a long time ago—without great customer service, you never can build a great company.

Right now, our big focus is customer service. We are making sure we are basically the best in customer service and trying to help everybody as much as we can as we grow with that email company.

STEPHANIE MULAC

MY NAME IS Stephanie Mulac, and I have been in the online world for probably about eight or nine years now. My family and I are very strong proponents of personal growth and self-improvement. My passion is helping others carve out the lifestyle of their dreams, and that's pretty much how I got into helping others online to do exactly what I do for a living.

Email marketing is truly the whole foundation of anything that we do online. It's what gives us an opportunity to reach out and connect with people—not just in our local communities or within a certain small geographic reach. It gives us the opportunity to reach people worldwide.

It wouldn't be possible without that list-building effort and without making a concerted effort to, not only build an email list, but to develop a rapport and to communicate with that list. That's the way we're able to reach out and impact the lives of hundreds of thousands and really make a difference with our message and communicating the passion that we have in life and what we want to bring to those online.

One of the first plans of action is list building. It's something that didn't exist years ago when I was first online. We had to do list building in a much more labor-intensive way and it was a much slower process.

It's being able to take advantage of an opportunity by purchasing solo ads. When you're able to do that, you are putting yourself in a position for absolutely the most rapid form of list building and being able to target the types of people that you're looking for.

It's being able to purchase solo ads from people who are already respected in their particular fields. So a recommendation from them to something that you have to offer comes with the highest regard and the highest trust factor.

You're immediately putting people on your list through buying solo ads who are going to be eager to get to know you and almost have an initial trust built in because they've been referred by somebody they already trust.

I think, for me, one of the most wonderful things about Clickonomy is it's an opportunity for people who are just getting started and want to get their feet wet, or are really in the early stages of building a huge , to connect with people who are experienced.

For me, personally, I really love to help people out. I love to see people get started on the right foot and not go through trial and error and get frustrated and go through years and years that they just don't seem to be getting the type of results that they're looking for.

Using something like Clickonomy, it is so gratifying to know people are able to present me with what it is that they want to share with the world. Then they, make a solo ad purchase, and know I'm able to share with my list the value that the people at Clickonomy are bringing to the table, and further improve that opportunity to spread the word and help people reach their personal development goals.

You're looking right now at my lifestyle. I'm sitting here doing this interview in my RV. It's a 40-foot motorhome, and I am parked about 10 minutes from DisneyWorld in Florida.

By having a list and by having the entire setup online to be able to sell my products and services, to be able to do lifestyle coaching with people, to be able to reach out through my list to make a difference in the lives of others—it also allows me to live the lifestyle of my dreams.

For eight years that has been traveling with my two daughters, homeschooling them, and traveling across the United States visiting more than 45 states at this point.

We literally go where we please, when we please, and have had the opportunity to see some amazing things throughout our entire country. That is truly the lifestyle of our dreams.

Because I have my list-building process and my email list in place and have the ability to reach out to people through that list and communicate with them, it gives me the opportunity to live that lifestyle while I am, in turn, being able to help others live the lifestyle of their dreams.

The best way to keep in touch with me is through stephaniemulac.com. I have products that are coming out all the time. I have a meditation series. I have a new series of brain wave entrainment audios— many, many different opportunities to connect with me and to make a difference in the lives of others.

Whether it's through affiliate marketing, solo ads at Clickonomy, or any number of ways—I'm always looking to help others and to make a difference.

ZANE BAKER

MY NAME IS Zane Baker and I am a full-time internet marketer. I actually have two businesses in two different niches.

One of them is 'personal development' and the other one is 'survival'. They are very different in nature, and I still was able to make it happen on the internet—in both niches.

I've been doing internet marketing for the past two years. I've been seeing major results in the past year or so, and I've been seeing great, great results in the past six months. Things have been transforming quite a lot for me and my business.

In the last six months, I have truly established myself as an authority in multiple platforms—which means I have a good-sized list. There are people out there with list-size in the hundreds of thousands. I'm still in the lower strata—between 10 and 15 thousand —but it's in two niches. So combined that's like 30,000 people.

I have two blogs in both niches, so that only drives more traffic to both my website and to my offers. And then on top of it, I just learned about solo ads in the past three or four months and that instead of me just buying solo ads, I can actually sell solo ads.

That has been amazing because I have a very, very good list and I nurture them really well. I give them really great content. So when somebody comes and buys a solo ad from me, they see results immediately because my lists are very responsive with what I put in front of them. But it took a long time to build that relationship with the list. When they learned who Zane Baker was and what he provided, they started clicking like crazy and it's awesome. I love that.

Email marketing is the key. Because even though I have multiple platforms like Facebook, my blog, everything else—the big results I see are from my email list because everything I do, I send it right to their inbox. They interact with me via email. Email is very personal, so when somebody trusts you and gives you their email, you need to treat it with respect.

When you do that, you will have a long-term relationship with the prospect. They will turn into customers, and they will turn into repeat customers. Internet marketing is the big picture, and email marketing is the main component in my business.

Their first plan of action for people who are just

starting out would be to know where their passion lies. They need to know which niche they will perform the best in. Once they figure out the niche they want, then it becomes really easy to get your foot in the door because you know your purpose.

So all you need to start doing is giving your content to people. This is really not hard to do, especially in today's technologically advanced market.

There are solo ads you can use to start a list. You can create a blog and drive people to sign up to your opt-in pages and create a list.

You can do Facebook advertising. There are so many ways you can do it. The time is now because you don't have to invest a lot of money like the old days where you literally needed thousands upon thousands of dollars. Right now, with a small budget you can start building a list and you can start seeing amazing results with even a small list of 500 to 1,000. As I said earlier, if you nurture your list, they will be very responsive.

The key is in having a responsive list. It doesn't matter how big or small it is. If they interact with your emails, if they click on your links, if they feel you are giving them great content—that's the key. I honestly believe anybody who is interested in internet marketing and wants to start a business, the time is now because it's a piece of cake.

The number one thing where Clickonomy stands out is you are protected both as a customer and as a buyer. I've used other platforms in the past, and I've been burnt. Clickonomy addressed that one area where a lot of other businesses haven't, and that's why I use Clickonomy exclusively—both when I buy click packages and sell click packages.

Because they do things other businesses don't. They do verifications, where they make sure the person is actually a person, or a business. They hold the funds in escrow, so you're not paying until you deliver. Especially for a customer who is new, and they have that doubt: "I don't know this person. How am I just going to pay him $500? What if he or she doesn't deliver?"

Clickonomy takes that out of the game because they will not pay the seller until they deliver. That protects the buyer.

You are protected as a seller also because you are verified. So Clickonomy knows you are a legitimate business and they protect you in case of fraud—they have your back.

Before I started *selling* clicks on Clickonomy, I *bought* multiple packages. I bought everything from a small 250 -package to as big as 5,000 clicks; I've tried it all and the results are fantastic.

When I started and didn't trust somebody, Clickonomy made it easier for me to make the decision. So that's my perspective as a buyer.

Now once I shifted gear and became a SELLER, I knew how other buyers were feeling because I was in their shoes not long ago. So I understand their fears, I understand their concerns, I understand their doubt.

So I used what I learned by being a buyer myself to teach the prospects who want to buy clicks from me. I told them how I built huge lists in less than three months and how right now, I am actually a seller.

So you could be the next me. You could buy clicks from me and other people on Clickonomy and build your own list and build your own existence. Then you turn around and become a seller yourself.

I've been on both parts as a seller and as a buyer —so this helps a lot. If you actually check my account you will see the raving reviews I'm getting from my customers because I was in their shoes and I felt... I still feel their fears and their concerns.

So when I deliver, my customers feel ecstatic because now the doubts are gone. Somebody has actually sold them clicks, they saw results and they were protected.

I have a PD list and I have a survivalist list and I'm selling clicks all the time on Clickonomy. I sell everything from 500 clicks all the way to 1,500. I'm working on expanding over the next three months to the 2,000- and 3,000-click packages. I'm doing my homework and I'm bringing it to everybody else in the next few months.

Email marketing actually is the number one area that has transformed my life, both personally and professionally. Because up until two months ago, I was actually in a 9 to 5 job.

And even though I loved my job and the work I did—because I was doing training and development, which is my passion—I felt stifled.

I felt like I was not helping as many people as I could, because I could only reach so many people being employed in a company. So internet marketing and email marketing has changed that for me dramatically.

I can reach those 30,000 people in my list and beyond. Every time I send an email to somebody, if the content I created was good, they will forward it to their friends, they will post it to their Facebook, they will put it on their Google+.

Internet marketing just ignited that passion in

me of helping others and, at the same time, it made it *easier* for me to deliver and help others online. Professionally it enabled me to become a networker, because I love people. I love to meet new people and I love to travel.

Internet marketing and email marketing has enabled me to do that because I don't have a 9 to 5 job. So I can attend seminars, I can attend webinars, I can attend live events, and all that just enables me to meet more people. I make more contacts, meet possible JV partners, and I mean, look at us now.

I am with you, on a Google Hangout, live. I can tell you I would not have been able to do that six months ago, sitting in my little office, responding to email or helping somebody deal with their career crisis.

But look at me now. I am sitting here freely in the comfort of my house, in my beautiful home office where I'm not distracted. I am not stressed about driving in the crazy traffic in D.C.

I know nobody knows that, but I live in D.C. and D.C.'s traffic is ridiculous. There's always a rush hour. It doesn't matter what time of the day, there is a rush hour.

Email marketing enabled me to become my true self, to help others and to truly transform my life and the life of others. So I thank email marketing and the people who created it. I thank the people who are still doing business in it because they are allowing me to take my place in the world and be able to help others.

AURELIJUS TERMINAS

I GOT STARTED in late 2012. I've been doing bits and pieces. I started with mostly free traffic methods: Twitter Marketing, Social Media, Facebook, Pinterest, all that kind of stuff.

I've learned from a lot of mistakes as many people in the internet marketing industry have.

I've been in ups and downs, all sorts of things happened. I nearly got sued by Tony Robbins last year.

Yeah, I had to learn all the things the hard way. I think, well, at least a couple of things—the copyrights and everything; just plain stupid mistakes. But when you go through those kinds of experiences, I think you become even stronger.

If you pick yourself up each time you fall, you are going to go a long way.

Nowadays, I do mostly paid advertising. I buy traffic. I buy solo ads. I buy Facebook traffic. I've got my own blog where I do videos and stuff, mostly in the personal development niche.

So that's how I started. I bought courses from

some top people in the social media industry back in 2012, but I've done a lot of changes. Some methods weren't effective anymore, so I had to switch to advertising, learned how to do Facebook ads, solo ads and stuff.

I started following top people in the solo ad industry. I started selling solo ads to people on Facebook.

There was like a big problem selling solo ads in my niche, particularly in the personal development niche.

I found a lot of people selling clicks in the internet marketing industry. I couldn't find anybody who wanted to buy clicks in the personal development field.

I use Clickonomy just to help me to boost my business. I think it was really needed, because you had brought in buyers from all types of niches: personal development, Forex, and all those other niches that aren't advertised that much online. You're a really big part of my business right now

I think Clickonomy is 90 percent of my business, and it's pretty scary at the moment if I lose my list. What I would do then?

You kind of need to spread it out—you can't put all your eggs in one basket. You need to double up other things like Facebook. You need to bring your audience maybe to your Facebook fan page.

Then you can communicate with them if GetResponse or server is down for a day or two.

But yeah, email marketing is huge. I think it's the most effective way to reach your audience, to basically do business online.

I don't know anyone in the internet marketing field who hasn't got a list of her own.

I mean, the people who own authority sites, perhaps, they argue that they don't need a list. But anyway, a list is a "must have" these days in internet marketing. I mean 90-95 percent of my business is email marketing.

There are plenty of list building courses out there. I think Anik has an amazing course. I think if you just grab that course, you'll have no problem whatsoever starting email marketing. It's really simple.

You learn all the bits and bots that make your email marketing business more effective.

There's tools, there's strategies, there's copy writing skills and all that kind of stuff.

But you'll learn that a long the way, so initially you can start doing it within days.

There's no big upfront cost compared to brick and mortar businesses. So, email marketing is really a way to start. You can just stand up, create a opt-in page, and start your business right now in minutes in what you simply excel in and test things out.

There are quite a few newbies on my buyers list. It depends how they treat the audience—the email follow-ups.

I review the opt-in pages. I review the offers. I just give some basic suggestions on how they can improve conversions, how they can improve the headlines and all that kind of stuff.

They normally experience really good results and, as you can see on my profile, most of the people are really happy with their results. I think like 95 percent or more give me positive feedback and it's all about testing things out.

You start with one headline on your opt-in pages. You test out different pages. You test out different headlines, and offers and everything else, and you just learn along the way.

I always try to help my customers with improving conversions, improving sales, and all that kind of stuff. So far, all good. No hard feelings or angry customers whatsoever, so that's good.

What is the email lifestyle? Well, basically my version of email lifestyle is freedom from—well, the location.

You can pick any city you want to live in, and basically you don't need to be attached to an office.

I started internet marketing because I wanted to travel. I can pick up my laptop, it's this idea of having freedom. You can just buy a plane ticket to go to your favourite place, sit at some coffee shop and work on your laptop. That was the dream. And I'm getting there.

I don't really care much about the fancy cars or everything else that is advertised through internet marketing, mansions or whatever.

You definitely can achieve that, but mostly it's all about the freedom that you don't need to answer to anyone. You can start really quickly. You basically can have your business up and running like in a couple of days. You will learn along the way and it's all about the freedom—the financial freedom.

You can seriously be financially secure if you have a pretty good and responsive list.

Within six months, I see people getting amazing results if they do their homework, if they keep improving and they keep learning. It's freedom from wherever you are. Freedom to live anywhere in the world. I think that's the biggest advantage of email marketing to me.

If I had to start all over again, I would buy

some traffic. I would build a page. I would build an offer. I would set up a funnel, and I think I would do things exactly as I'm doing them right now.

I would buy some traffic, buy some solo ads, buy clicks from Clickonomy perhaps, or Facebook traffic, Twitter ads, media buys, whatever, you know.

It's just a matter of time.

How much time you're going to invest in that?

So we'll invest the profits, build a list, and more money, you know, and recuperate the losses. I have had to rebuild my list a couple of times already. So it's been rebuilt successfully, so it's just a matter of time right now.

I had this idea before I started email marketing that I wanted to write a book about business and psychology. So that's the main reason why I chose a person to work on the field when I started internet marketing. I loved the idea of Tony Robbins—big performance coaching stuff that you need to attend if you want to make money. If you want to change your lifestyle, change your habits.

You need to have the right psychology, the right mind-set. I want to talk about that in my own book. I want to have something for my own story. How I started; how I flopped a few times; how I had my ups and downs.

So yeah, it's my little baby that I'm working on. I hope I will be able to get it out in a couple of years' time. I'm still working on the plan and everything else and have my initial transcript. But yeah, that book is what is driving me every day to work harder on my business.

I don't think email marketing will be my last venture. I think it's just initial start-up.

I have ideas for other projects. I'm seeing myself in the business world and email marketing is really the initial step up in the business. Because these days, internet has become such an easy way to start something of your own.

PART FOUR
The Future

NEXT UP

YOU ARE AWESOME! You have almost finished this book and that, in itself, shows you're serious about setting up your own awesome email marketing business. I hope my story and the stories of all the other marketers in this book have inspired you in some way to take action.

I've taught more than 25,000 people and the one complaint I have with most of my students is they don't take action. There's WAY too much information out there to get lost and so will you if you don't stop, focus, and start working.

Once you have a plan, and that plan sounds good to you—implement that plan. Work on it as hard as you can. Online business is very different from a traditional business and the amount of automation you can achieve with your online business is remarkable.

Some of my students simply set up completely automated funnels. Yes, they even outsource their email writing process—and it works for them. I don't recommend you start outsourcing every part of your

business from the get-go. What I do recommend is—
start your hustle. Not tomorrow. Not next week.
Today.

Make a promise. No, make a commitment.
You are your own witness. You have thought about
changing your life for your entire life. It's time to stop
thinking and start doing.

I have given you a solid plan, which, if
implemented properly can yield multiple profitable
long-term funnels—all of which add to your bottom
line.

I've mentioned all of the tools I personally use
in my business and I suggest you start using them
yourself. They will make your life a whole lot easier
and when that happens—your chances of quitting will
drastically decrease.

Some awesome technologies are out there—
opt-in page creation, driving traffic, split testing,
sending autoresponders, and email analytics. Learn
those technologies. If you're thinking it will take you
weeks to learn everything, you're wrong.

When you start your hustle—which is today—
you will realize everything that looks complicated
right now will slowly pave the way to become essential
tools in your business.

New and awesome opt-in page templates

coming out every week. New features being built in Clickonomy every day. Email deliverability is improving.

More and more people are getting into the email marketing business. And today—it's your turn.

EMAIL INSTRUMENTS

CONGRATULATIONS! IF YOU follow the steps mentioned in this book, you will be well on your way to becoming an email marketing ninja.

My goal with this book was to highlight the importance of email marketing and why I believe it is one of the BEST ways to get started with an online business.

I have some great news for you if you're ready and willing to take action.

I've created an amazing membership program on the Email Instruments strategy, which includes video training, screen sharing, whiteboard sessions, free traffic, free autoresponder account, expert interviews and a whole lot more.

Listen, I want you to become a success story. And with the Email Instruments membership, you will literally get everything you need to start your email marketing business in one place. And then some.

So if you're ready, go to this link and let's get started: https://emailinstruments.com

Printed in Great Britain
by Amazon

46756362R00102